Praise for *EDrenaline RUSH*

"More than any other teacher I know, John Meehan embodies the idea of the teacher as a transformational figure. He is devoted to making the classroom a place where students matter... love of learning can come alive. We're ... so ... ugh to put his ideas between covers. ... John (and a book like this) when I was ... have quit."

—Greg To..., senior editor at *Inside Higher Ed*, author of *The Game Believes in You*

"John Meehan has figured out how to come up with a creative activity for almost any kind of content or skill you want your students to acquire, and he has listed them all here. This easy-to-read, entertaining book can be read cover to cover or flipped to any random page; either way, you're bound to come away with a great idea or three. It's packed with practical tips and great writing that will have you coming back for more of his dynamic, rigorous approach to classroom teaching."

—Alexis Wiggins, teacher, and author of
The Best Class You Never Taught

"*EDrenaline Rush* walks the reader down a path straight to creative freedom and joy-filled lessons. John has masterfully captured the inspiration in vignettes from life moments that rouse us to action in our classrooms. This is a must-buy and should be a must-implement for everyone who wants to create positive change in their schools."

—Michael Matera, teacher, and author of *eXPlore Like a Pirate*

"Why do humans like amusement parks, mud runs, and escape rooms? Because they are exciting, fun, and there's an element of heart-pounding thrill associated with them. So why can't our lessons and classrooms be like them? They absolutely can, and John Meehan takes you through the experience as if you were on a ride, in a run, or looking to escape the room. His examples will energize you and make you rethink how you design and teach lessons to your students. Every classroom can be filled with 'student-centered adrenaline,' and after reading *EDrenaline Rush*, you will be motivated to make it happen."

—Scott Rocco, EdD, Hamilton Township, New Jersey School District
Superintendent, #satchat co-founder, co-author of
140 Twitter Tips for Educators and *Hacking Google for Education*

"I saw John Meehan's #QRBreakIN activities on Twitter and was hooked. The idea was brilliant: Identify something students would learn. Infuse it with themes from a board game or video game they love. Break it up into several small challenges. Make learning a game! Your students will thank you!"

—**Matt Miller**, veteran teacher, blogger, and
author of *Ditch That Textbook*

"*EDrenaline Rush* is the ultimate surprise and delight! As an educator for students of all ages, this is a must-read book! I was inspired all over again to search for that 'one little spark.' Meehan's enthusiasm is infectious, and if we could bottle John's energy and determination to eradicate boring learning, I have no doubt we could change the game of education everywhere!"

—**Monica Cornetti**, CEO Sententia Gamification,
GamiCon Gamemaster

"A lot of people like to talk about ways to get more students engaged in deep learning, but few are willing to offer specific examples of how to make that happen. What Meehan has done in his brilliant book, *EDrenaline Rush*, is put a treasure trove of gamified course materials out there for all to see. He is not hiding his pedagogy and approach as if it were some kind of secret sauce—he is willing to put it all out there so others can use, critique, or remix it as they see fit. When we actively share innovative models of teaching and learning that work, we allow others to refine, validate, and scale those ideas so that they positively impact other schools and students. That is precisely what Meehan has done in this go-to resource for the gamified classroom."

—**Ben Owens**, former STEM Teacher, Open Way Learning
consultant, and author of *Open Up, Education!*

"The moment I started reading, I knew this was a book I would devour. John beautifully weaves his personal and classroom adventures, clearly illustrating how easily we can create our own epic educational experiences. From beginning to end, *EDrenaline Rush* provides exactly as the title suggests. You will come away energized, inspired, and with a rush of *EDrenaline* that will launch you into your own epic adventure! This book is for everyone and is one that you will refer to repeatedly for ideas and inspiration. A must-read!"

—**Tisha Richmond**, tech integrations specialist, author of *Make Learning Magical*

"*EDrenaline Rush* catalyzes and stimulates any teacher's natural urge to authentically engage students through active learning. John's vibrant writing mirrors his classroom culture and personal demeanor—high energy! In *EDrenaline Rush*, John welcomes teachers to engage with him with easily digestible how-tos that create dynamic experiences that can transform any classroom into a stealth learning zone. Whether you are simply curious about gamifying learning or well along the journey to transform your learning community, *EDrenaline Rush* has something for you. With a menu of empowering ideas and activities, you will not be bored reading this fast-paced book."

—**Nathan Strenge**, teacher and school designer

"*EDrenaline Rush* surprised me not only by the sheer volume of ideas for classroom engagement but also for being an instrument to transmit John's passion, enthusiasm, and energy around the topic. If you're looking for a book that gets you excited and provides lots of ideas and examples to implement in your classroom, you've found it!"

—**Rob Alvarez**, teacher, international keynote speaker, and host of the *Professor Game* podcast

Game-changing Student Engagement Inspired
by Theme Parks, Mud Runs, and Escape Rooms

John Meehan

Published by Dave Burgess Consulting, Inc.
San Diego, CA
DaveBurgessConsulting.com

Cover Design by Genesis Kohler
Editing and Interior Design by My Writers' Connection

Library of Congress Control Number: 2019940277
Paperback ISBN: 978-1-949595-38-3
Ebook ISBN: 978-1-949595-39-0

First Printing: May 2019

Dedication

To Laura.

For driving me to be stronger and
teaching me how to drive.

Love you like crazy.

Contents

Foreword

I think about it often. I was only a few months into my first year as an elementary principal at the ripe old age of thirty, and I was about to have "the talk" with my entire staff. I wasn't unaccustomed to uncomfortable conversations with people. For the past two years, I'd been an assistant principal and had the opportunity to work with a super amazing principal who taught me the ways of leadership.

But this talk was a little bit different. I had been a student many years ago at the very school where I was now principal. Within the community, it was considered "the" school to attend, and it's the kind of place where teachers get hired and never leave until retirement. It was (and still is) an amazing place for kids, but I knew we could be better. So it was time for the talk.

Teachers gathered for the monthly staff meeting, and even though we'd only been together for a few months, there was already a routine and some expectation as to how things would go. But as teachers rolled in and got settled, they could tell this meeting would be different.

I stood in silence for a few moments. Not that awkward silence when people aren't sure what to say and get uncomfortable; it was more of a "he has something important to say" kind of silence. What I was about to say wasn't actually a huge problem at the school. Parents weren't complaining. Students still liked school. But I'm a firm believer that if you see something happening and you know better, you should speak up and say something. So I did.

I talked with my teachers about some of the students we all knew who were struggling at school and even more so with their homelives. We talked about the children who were in foster care and bouncing around different homes and feeling very unsettled in their lives. We talked about the kids who always seemed cheerful and happy at school, even when something not so great was happening at home.

We also talked about those kids who just didn't *get* school. They would come every day, sit compliantly, and do some work, but they were not "experiencing" their educational journey the way they could and should have been. Many of those were also the ones who learned differently from their peers; they didn't necessarily need more; they just needed something a little bit different.

I talked, and my teachers listened. We all got choked up. And then I gave an ultimatum: "We as the adults have bad days; everyone does. But it's not fair to our students if we impose our bad days on them. So from this day forward, we're only going to have good and great days—period. Our kids deserve our best every single day because you never truly know what each of them is going through in their lives."

"We're going to be positive, happy, outgoing, and even on our worst days, still be the best we can for our kids with a good or great day. We're not going to just come to school and give worksheets or assign pages in the math book. Creating an engaging school experience is what we are going to do. There will be times when the journey will be hard, but anything worth doing in life is hard. And the outcome is even sweeter once the journey is over."

From that day forward, the school changed. The community could feel it, and so could our students. Nobody just *did* school;

we created an experience. That was the best "talk" I ever decided to have. We made some powerful changes, but I *wish* this book would have been available as a resource for my teachers back then.

I predict that *EDrenaline Rush* will be a game changer for schools and districts across the country. I've come to believe that John is my BFAM (brother from another mother). We share the same belief that our students deserve our best—every day. (I highly doubt that John can even say the word mediocre.)

What you're about to experience in this literary gem is second to none in terms of inspiration and practical information. You're going to be challenged to rethink the learning experiences you offer students. The number and variety of ideas you're going to read about is going to blow you away. You won't be able to help being motivated to always come to school and make it either a good or great day for your students.

What you're about to experience is high-octane amazingness for teachers and students everywhere. Buckle up! Lace up your shoes, charge your devices, put on your Disney T-shirts, and don't forget to hydrate, because the *EDrenaline Rush* experience begins now! I'm going with John. Will you join us?

Adam Welcome
coauthor of *Kids Deserve It!* and author of *Run Like a Pirate*

Origin Stories

Every January, my family makes an annual trek down to Walt Disney World in Orlando, Florida. Truth be told, I guess you could say we are one of those "Disney families," but the real reason we make the trip is in honor of my Aunt Judi, the founder of an educational software company who's spent the better part of the last four decades helping struggling students learn how to read. She is a warrior, a philanthropist, and truly a phenomenal human being in her own right, who has dedicated her life to the service and support of students with learning disabilities (including kids with dyslexia like me!). But in 2010, my Aunt Judi was diagnosed with breast cancer, and our family was devastated.

How do you pay tribute to someone who's done so much for so many? (Because let's be honest; when you're trying to find the perfect way to honor the CEO of a software company, cards and flowers kind of fall short.)

Answer: You convince your entire family to run a marathon.

For the past ten years or so, members of my extended family (moms, dads, aunts, uncles, and cousins) make the trip down to

Orlando to take part in the events surrounding the annual Walt Disney World Marathon—the largest weekend running festival in the country, with proceeds benefiting the Leukemia & Lymphoma Society. Some of my youngest second cousins, older aunts, and uncles started out by running the "Mickey Mile" or the Family 5K. The more "goofy" among us twenty- and thirty-somethings typically run some combination of the 10K, the half marathon, the full marathon, a two-day combo race, or the full slate of events for just under fifty miles in four days and the right to call yourself a proud owner of the coveted "Dopey Challenge" medal. Some years ago, I even convinced my wife, Laura, to join me in racing the half marathon, figuring it would be a one-off event since—in her own words—she hates running. Half a decade later, she's run four Disney marathons *and* a 39.3-mile Goofy Challenge. And my Aunt Judi's cancer is in complete remission.

The Disney race weekend is a good example of just how easy it is to lose yourself in a world of escapism and fantasy. As your heart pounds and your adrenaline pumps, it's hard not to get caught up in the sheer force of positive energy from costumed characters lining the streets and the thousands of strangers cheering every step you take. It's almost no wonder that the race weekend attracts approximately 50,000 runners every year. As Disney puts it, when you're running there, "every mile is magic." It's awe-inspiring to see the incredible lengths to which people are able to push themselves when they're able to look past the fact that they're actually putting forth a *ton* of really hard work.

You really do start to feel like you're invincible.

So there's the end of that story and the beginning of another one.

I teach two sections of American literature and serve as the instructional coach for a high school of about 1,100 students and 101 teachers in Arlington, Virginia. Classroom teaching alone keeps me incredibly busy, but the life of an instructional coach pretty much boils down to a never-ending game of academic Whac-A-Mole to keep a finger on the pulse of where the best practices are shaping classrooms across the country. In an era of 24/7 information, great ideas can come from just about anywhere: books, blogs, social media, YouTube, even popular TV shows and movies. For instructional coaches, gathering and sharing ideas usually means spending a lot of time on Twitter listening in on teaching conversations, reading tons of books to plan and study professional development (PD), browsing teacher podcasts and professional publications to keep tabs on current research, and talking shop at conferences to stay on top of the latest trends in education.

In November of 2017, I traveled to Williamsburg for the annual Virginia Association for Supervision and Curriculum

Development (VASCD) conference to deliver a presentation on adapting fantasy sports into the classroom. There, I had the chance to hear the keynote speaker, George Couros, give a presentation inspired by his book, *The Innovator's Mindset*. Being a professional development nerd, I figured I might as well pick up a copy of his book before the event and tweet out ideas and inspiration.

Twitter Works!

Like a total teacher fanboy, I asked George to take a selfie with me just before his presentation, so I could add it to my collection of photos taken with education rockstars like Todd Whitaker and Carol Dweck. As I sheepishly approached George at the front of the room, fumbling over how I might even start a conversation, he may or may not have greeted me with a big, friendly, Canadian smile, saying: "Hey you're John! From Twitter! The stuff you're doing on Twitter is amazing, and I'm so honored to meet you." Dreams come true, kids!

Fast-forward to December. My wife Laura and I were packing for a two-week winter break where we would travel with her entire family to visit my sister-in-law in Nuremberg, Germany. To make better (and more interesting) use of the time it took to pack my bags for the long trip, I fired up a few videos from Matt Miller's *Ditch That Textbook* digital summit. (I told you I am a PD nerd.) One of the videos was a presentation by author Michael Matera, the gamification guru behind the book *eXPlore Like a Pirate*.

What struck me most about Michael's session was just how firmly grounded in a human-centered design and sound educational research his message and practice of gamification were. More than just fun and games, Michael's presentation left me feeling energized and full of countless ideas for my own classroom. Just like my family's upcoming annual Disney trip, this guy had me

Connect with me! @MeehanEDU

looking beyond Christmas break to something *fun!* So as I finished packing the last of my things for the transatlantic flight, I downloaded a copy of his book.

The funny thing about long plane rides is you really don't have much time to do anything else besides read, sleep, and think. Without a steady Wi-Fi connection at 35,000 feet, I really didn't have much else to do other than spend some time hopping back and forth between a handful of books that I had loaded onto my Kindle for the trip: Daniel Pink's *Drive*, Neal Gabler's biography of Walt Disney, George Couros' *The Innovator's Mindset* (which the teachers in my department were reading as part of a book group), and Michael Matera's *eXPlore Like a Pirate*. By the time Laura and I had landed in Nuremberg by way of Vienna by way of Dublin (Hey look, two teacher salaries can only make international flights happen with budget airlines and connecting flights!), the high-altitude cocktail of educational adrenaline had mixed together enough to inspire about 90 percent of the book that you are reading today. When we made it back to the States and landed in Disney for our annual marathon weekend, all the pieces of the puzzle fell into place. As I made my way through the packed runner's expo hall to pick up my race bib and timing chip, I felt a palpable energy surging through the entire arena. It was then that I noticed a distinct pattern that connected the thousands of runners at the race expo and the words of inspiration I'd been reading over the holiday break.

Everywhere I looked, there was a sea of weekend warriors, aspiring athletes, and total strangers decked out in their Disney finest, eagerly anticipating the race events that were to come. I couldn't help but feel overwhelmed by the stories of so many of these runners as they beamed with positive energy and prepared to tackle feats that bordered on the impossible. Runners were sporting homemade T-shirts, signs, mementos, and banners with the faces and names of loved ones:

"I'm running for my Aunt Judi!"

"I'm running in memory of my dad!"

"Running for two. Little runner due this summer!"

"I'm racing for a cure."

"Racing in remission! It's my first marathon!"

"Proud supporter of Team in Training and the fight against Leukemia & Lymphoma."

My energy soared as I soaked in the incredible excitement that surrounded me. As Walt Disney himself so famously said: "It's kind of fun to do the impossible!" And at the height of a full-blown educational adrenaline rush, I drafted an email to the pirate captain himself, the one and only Mr. Dave Burgess, with this wild idea for a book.

In *Teach Like a Pirate,* Dave writes,

> *For many students, school is filled with monotony, drudgery, and soul-killing suckiness. When I think about a student's typical school day, it makes me completely understand why so many of them don't want to be there. Too often school is a place where creativity is systematically killed, individuality is stamped out, and boredom reigns supreme. There are really only two possibilities; either your class can be a reprieve from all of that or it can be a contributing factor. I am thoroughly committed to having my class be a reprieve.*

I couldn't agree more.

As I stood, surrounded by 50,000 runners sharing stories of heartache and willpower as they prepared to attempt incredible feats well beyond ordinary limits, it was hard not to get emotional. I thought about all the countless teachers and students in schools and classrooms around the country who greet everyday academia with a sense of drudgery, all the while bravely shouldering their own private burdens, healing from their own personal trauma, and working through their own very real fears, doubts, and struggles. Learning disabilities. Loss of loved ones. Breakups. Battles with cancer. Bullying. Body shaming. Self-harm. FOMO. Social Media overload. Anxiety. Depression. I couldn't help but think: *Isn't the 'real world' hard enough? There's got to be a way to make education fun.*

How much more would we learn if going to school felt more like going to an amusement park? Could classroom activities elicit the same sense of exhilaration you feel when charging a hill in a marathon or a mud run? And how much safer and more supported

Proudly sporting Mickey Mouse medals and Mylar blankets with my cousins Ted and Mariana after our family's first Disney Marathon. See the pink KT tape on my hand? That's for my Aunt Judi.

would students feel about their own education if every day was filled with the same sort of mystery and mastery you would expect from a twisting escape room of puzzles and surprises?

Serious academics might laugh at the notion. But twentieth-century German Catholic philosopher Josef Pieper, one of the most noteworthy St. Thomas Aquinas scholars in history, reminds us that this crazy notion of injecting more "fun" in schools actually has roots dating way back to antiquity. In his landmark 1952 text, *Leisure: The Basis of Culture,* Pieper explains:

It is essential to begin by reckoning with the fact that one of the foundations of Western culture is leisure (...) And even the history of the word attests the fact: for leisure in Greek is skole, and in Latin scola, the English "school." The word used to designate the place where we educate and teach is derived from a word which means "leisure." "School" does not, properly speaking, mean school, but leisure.

Yet somewhere along the line—perhaps, as noted historian Howard Zinn suggests in *A People's History of the United States*, around the time of the Industrial Revolution—schools gradually started to champion cold efficiency over leisure. By the mid-1800s, Mark Twain was writing schoolhouse horror stories where daydreamers like Tom Sawyer regularly ran afoul of stern-faced instructors. By the early 1900s, the shift had become so entrenched in the American education system that most institutions literally whipped, paddled, or shamed children into compliance, transforming schools into little more than a sort of junior version of overcrowded factory floors and low-wage assembly lines. And even today, schools everywhere are eliminating recess, downsizing art and music departments, and slashing budgets by eliminating "leisurely" extracurricular programs–all while reporting unprecedented levels of teacher burnout and student stress.

How did an entire system lose sight of its intended purpose? There's an old saying in teaching that you can't take it personally. But I firmly disagree: Our job as educators affords us the incredible opportunity to deal firsthand with the hopes, dreams, fears, aspirations, doubts, joys, setbacks, struggles, and triumphs of real, live human beings. That's every bit as much of the "real world" for our students as the narrow curriculum that any course might ever hope to cover in 180 days. You'd better believe I take this job personally! And that's why I'm committed to putting my whole self into it—and to helping my students discover the world-changing potential that each of them holds by charging headlong into whatever challenges might lie in their paths to take authentic ownership of their own educations. The big secret of all teaching boils down to this: We don't teach content. We use course content to teach people. It simply doesn't get more personal than that.

We don't teach content. We use course content to teach people.

There's another saying in education that goes like this: *Your favorite class is the one you like the most. Your best class is the one in which you learn the most.* I want my class to be both of those things. Every. Single. Day.

So paragraphs turned into pages, and I kept writing. Part educational treatise melding a decade of classroom experience with some 36,000 miles of conference travel for instructional coaching. Part vacation guide from a lifelong theme-park junkie. And part training regimen from a thrill-seeker with a flair for the extreme. The idea for this book was to talk about all the things that theme parks, mud runs, and escape rooms do right. I wanted to help teachers and students enter what Samuel Taylor Coleridge would call "a willful suspension of disbelief." What Hungarian psychologist Mihaly Csikszentmihalyi would call the "flow state"—that mental state of operation in which a person performing an activity is fully immersed in a feeling of energized focus, full involvement, and enjoyment in the process. Or what Dutch historian Johan Huizinga might call that elusive "magic circle," where the rules of the outside world don't apply to the rules of the game. I wanted to dig deep into three of my own great passions and talk about how educators can adapt those very same principles into their classrooms to create richly themed worlds of wonder, excitement, and student-centered adrenaline.

If the Disney races have taught me anything, it's that high energy "fun and games" can be a Trojan Horse for getting folks so fired up that they can't wait to tackle some seriously impressive work. I want to empower teachers to treat lesson planning like a more fluid and dynamic "game plan," where high-energy student learning is always at the center of the action. And I want my students to feel invincible from the second they set foot in the room.

The world outside of school is hard enough. And while I unquestionably want my classroom to prepare students for all the tough stuff that life will throw at them, I absolutely want my learners to feel safe, supported, and excited to be there every single day. Theme parks and roller coasters are thrilling, but you are very rarely—if ever—in any real danger. Mud runs are wild, but race officials are there to help you every step of the way. Escape rooms are full of high-pressure situations and peril, but you're only ever a moment away from a major breakthrough and the next vital clue to cracking the code. Like any good game, the key to a truly engaging classroom is to have fun while still playing it S.A.F.E., by crafting every high-energy lesson in such a way that it delivers:

- Specific
- Actionable
- Feedback
- Expediently

I want my classroom to feel like *that*.

In the immortal words of Dave Burgess, teachers should be able to sell tickets to their lessons. This book is divided into three "big ticket" sections accordingly. And like any great theme park, you're welcome to explore these attractions in any order you'd like:

Welcome to an education tour-de-force that blends Disney-inspired classroom *imagineering* with student-centered instruction and pulse-pounding pedagogy, designed to add fun and excitement to any course or content area. What better name could there be for such a book than *EDrenaline Rush*?

Classroom teachers have such an incredible opportunity to shape the lives and futures of the students we serve. We have the power to light the fire in their eyes and help them achieve the impossible. So as we begin this adventure together, I remain humbled and inspired by the words of American novelist John Steinbeck, who, in a poem titled "Like Captured Fireflies," famously called himself "the unsigned manuscript" of his own high school English teacher, adding, "What deathless power lies in the hands of such a person."

Teaching is neither a lucrative nor a glamorous profession. But it is honest work and work worth doing to the very best of our abilities. From the bottom of my heart, I thank you for your passion and for your commitment to the incredible work that we do. I hope you'll join me in the mission to inspire that same spirit that Steinbeck so eloquently recalls from his own education: "a new attitude, a new hunger." Chase it. Embrace it. And let's change the game together.

I warmly invite you to connect with me and fellow readers on social media as we continue this conversation and conquer whatever obstacles might lie in our way using the hashtag #EDrenaline.

Let's do this.

PART I:

Theme Parks

*It's kind of fun to do
the impossible.*

—Walt Disney

Chapter 1

The Transformational Power of Theme

Film, entertainment, and animation pioneer Walt Disney was a master of world-building. Each year, millions of visitors flock to Disney theme parks from China to France. In 2014, *Forbes* magazine reported, "Theme parks are core to the business model of American media giant the Walt Disney Company. Last year its eleven parks around the world provided nearly a third of its $45 billion revenue and 20.7 percent of its $10.7 billion operating profit."

Nine of the ten most visited theme parks on the planet are run by Disney. The Magic Kingdom, the original theme park of The Walt Disney World Resort outside Orlando, Florida, boasts an attendance of more than 20 million guests annually, making it the single most popular theme park destination in the entire world.

Even though visitors to these fantasy lands know that they are not actually traveling aboard an interstellar rocket on Space Mountain or exploring a spooky haunted mansion full of "999 happy haunts," elaborately themed attractions are the secret ingredient to the world-famous "Disney Magic." The Disney Institute, the company's corporate training wing, writes at length about the Mouse House's fanatical attention to detail in the 2011 Disney

Institute book *Be Our Guest: Perfecting the Art of Customer Service.*
The corporation's customer service mantra is distilled into four
simple words: "At Disney, everything speaks."

From the number of steps between trash cans (thirty), to the
"forced perspective" technique that is used to make an iconic castle appear to be nearly twice its actual size (one-hundred-eighty-
three-feet tall), to the underground utilidor tunnels designed to
ensure that you'll never see two Mickey Mouses in the same place
at the same time, Disney's incredible attention to detail keeps cus-
tomers happy and immersed in their fantasy kingdom. That's why
it's called a "theme" park!

Imagine how much more our students might learn if we could
capture that same spirit of wonder and excitement in a classroom.

Once Upon a Dream

The Disney parks offer richly themed worlds and colorful characters, imbuing each space with a larger-than-life sense of setting, purpose, and place. As guests make their way through the entrance gates, a commemorative plaque greets them with the same welcome that was delivered by Walt Disney himself on the opening day of Disneyland: "Here You Leave Today And Enter The World Of Yesterday, Tomorrow And Fantasy." As Samuel Taylor Coleridge once wrote, walking into these parks, people step into the "willful suspension of disbelief." Guests feel as if they are entering into the story when they take their first steps into these timeless realms of imagination.

So what is the story of your classroom?

Before you answer that question, let's get clear about the small but crucial difference between a *story* and a *narrative*. A narrative is an open-ended string of events, unfolding at random in a loosely episodic string of "and then… and then… and then…" Sure, there are plenty of flashes of fun, fright, suspense, and surprise to be had along the way in any narrative. But more often than not, they leave you with a big old pile of stuff where things just sort of happen. Despite teachers' best efforts to make each day memorable, "Third grade," "Geometry," and "AP Euro" are narratives, not stories.

Lots of amusement parks offer thrills and spills without a story. Take, for example, your average amusement park's log flume: You hop in a boat, get hauled up a waterslide, and *whoosh*! Smile for the camera as you splash down for the perfect way to cool off on a hot summer day. Fun? No question. But what's the *story* here? Is a world-class log flume really enough to attract 20 million visitors a year? Not hardly.

In contrast to a narrative, a *story* has a clear beginning, a clear middle, and a definitive end. As Robert McKee, former professor at the University of Southern California and creator of the noted "Story Seminar" explains, a story tells the singular tale of an iconic hero in a journey against a clearly defined obstacle. Stories promise adventure through challenges that raise the stakes, where consequences topple like dominoes in a race against the clock. In the best story, you can't help but feel a mounting sense of excitement, where each stage of the journey proceeds "and so . . . and so . . . until finally . . . " and there's no place left to go but an ultimate showdown.

When you peel back the pixie dust, Disney's Splash Mountain is just a glorified log flume where you climb inside a floating ride vehicle and quickly sail past an audio-animatronic Br'er Rabbit, who you see boarding up his beloved family home in the briar patch and setting out to seek adventure on the open road. Yet during the next ten minutes, you follow our hero as he waves goodbye to his neighborhood with a quick spritz down Slippin' Falls, then tumble into the song-filled tunnels of his "Laughin' Place," and survive a close call with the villainous Br'er Fox and Br'er Bear before you are ultimately captured by this dastardly duo. As the music swells and darkness closes in around you, you see a pair of menacing vultures taunting your final ascent while Br'er Rabbit pleads with his captors not to be thrown into the briar patch! One high-energy, forty-five-degree angle drop later, and you're soaking wet, singing "Zip-a-Dee-Doo-Dah" with Br'er Rabbit and his friends from the safety of his briar patch home sweet home.

The narrative of both log flumes—climb into a boat, go up a conveyor belt, go down a water slide, get wet—is exactly the same. But the *story*? Wow.

These days, my eleventh grade English course is a 400(ish)-year survey of the major figures, time periods, and literary movements in American literature. As is often the case in survey courses, we move at a pretty healthy clip, so it's a challenge for students to keep track of just what, exactly, they're expected to do as we zip through approximately a decade's worth of American literature each week. In short, it's a narrative. Lots of stuff just sort of happens. Sure, I understand how it all connects, but it can be a real challenge for students to keep track of where "Romanticism" ends and "Realism" begins.

Back at The Magic Kingdom, every little detail, from the plant life to the architecture to the paving stones beneath your feet and the typefaces used on the signage, helps to carve the theme park into easily distinguishable "lands," like the rough-and-tumble "Adventureland" and the sleek and retro-futuristic "Tomorrowland." Each land has its own story with its unique sense of place and purpose. To lend cohesion to each of these disparate tales, the iconic castle sits at the dead center of the park. The lands stem from the central hub, almost as if the magical castle itself brings each of these new worlds to life.

So what if we turned 400 years of American literature into a yearlong chase for the American dream?

With a little help from iMovie, that's exactly the theme I created. Every new three-week-long unit is a new story, complete with full-color handouts, theme-park icons to guide the way, and a final challenge at the end. With planning and few details, each unit/story really starts to feel like its own little "land" inside of the larger, content-inspired universe that's just waiting to be discovered.

Tip: TheNounProject.com is excellent for icons, and my favorite site for free stock photos is Pexels.com.

With planning and few details, each unit/story really starts to feel like its own little "land" inside of the larger, content-inspired universe that's just waiting to be discovered.

Once you've nailed down your basic hub and spoke design, consider posting an oversized "park map" on a wall to help students keep visual track of the progress they're making throughout the year. Then invite them to co-create the world they're exploring by adding additional "points of interest" as your yearlong story unfolds.

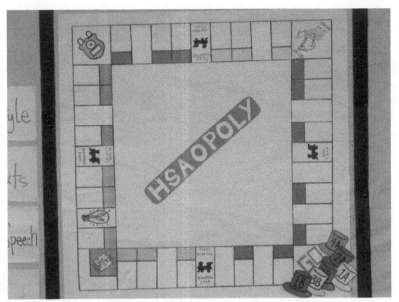

Here's the story of my tenth-grade class at Crossland High School: Four quarters of short fiction, rhetoric, poetry, and non-fiction study to prepare for the year-end High School Achievement exam. Each week, we'd fill in game board squares with newly covered content and move our class tokens one step closer to one of the four corners of the board (where we'd take our quarterly benchmark exams).

Off to Work We Go!

From your first step through the turnstiles, Disney parks use the power of storytelling to whisk guests away into magical worlds of imagination and wonder. Far too often, however, most school years begin with an awkward round of perfunctory icebreakers, followed by the usual low-energy parade of rules, procedures, and housekeeping items before making a clunky segue into course content.

Hard pass.

READY TO BLAST THROUGH THE PAST?

 Visit any one of the ten game stations to collect inventory items. There are ten inventory items to discover, and you can gather them in any order by accomplishing the task related to that game station.

 Talk with your teammates and check in with the Control Center to update them on your progress. Some games require teamwork!

 Once you've earned an inventory item, head to the Control Center. If it's good to go, update your progress on the overhead leaderboard!

 You'll have until the end of Friday's class to complete your item collection, so plan your time wisely! Once you've collected all ten items, submit your character sheet to the Control Center.

I want my students talking about my class at the dinner table from *the very first night* of school! And I want my yearlong story to spring to life from the moment students set foot in my classroom. With that goal in mind, we kick off our year-long chase for the American Dream as five competing teams of "time travelers" racing to "load our supplies" by completing ten different activities before the end-of-class bell rings. Instead of wasting time being talked at in compliant rows, student teams navigate activity stations in any order they'd like as if they were touring a theme park, getting hands-on practice with a mix of new school edtech and old school pedagogies like collaborative learning and honest-to-goodness *human interaction*, all of which are so critically important, especially in those early days of school. By the end of our first class period, students will have jumped right into the world of our year-long story by . . .

- Signing up to receive regular text message alerts
- Learning the ropes of the classroom with self-directed autonomy
- Completing course intro surveys to help me know who's who
- Recording short video introductions to give me a sense of their tech savvy
- Chatting with me casually without interrupting other teams' progress
- Posting selfies and bite-sized bios to help me put a face to a name
- Submitting goals and short writing samples to gauge the work that lies ahead

As Mary Poppins might say, "A spoonful of sugar helps the medicine go down." A clever bit of theming can get your students working, thinking, laughing, and *engaging* from the very moment class begins until long after the final bell has sounded for the day's instruction. Get the adrenaline pumping early, and students will leave excited to come back to see what you have in store for tomorrow.

Download and customize your own copies of these themed welcome activities at EDrenalineRush.com/ Resources.

It Was All Started By a Mouse

You don't need Disney dollars for high-impact theming. In spite of the incredible success that he would go on to achieve, Walt remained humble, famously reminding people that "it was all started by a mouse." Sometimes, a little creativity can go a long way!

My first teaching assignment was in an urban achievement gap high school just outside of Washington, D.C., where class sizes routinely exceeded thirty students, and approximately two out of three students qualified for free or reduced meals. As a new teacher, I taught six separate sections of sophomore English. The goal was to prepare these students to take the state-mandated High School Assessment (HSA) exam at the end of the year, but pass rates in that county were notoriously well below state averages. As a brand-new teacher in a school with incredibly limited resources, I had no money, no technology, and very little in the way of formal classroom experience. All I knew was that I'd been tasked with getting more than 200 (yes, 200) students from a high-needs population in a failing school system to pass the HSA exam.

Because it felt like one epic episode of *Mission: Impossible*, I used a giant piece of old cardboard to create a massive sign that I hung in the front of my room. It read: "CLASSIFIED INFORMATION: TOP SECRET!"

For the first week of school, students wondered about the sign as we went through the usual back-to-school routine: rules, procedures, consequences, icebreakers, signed copies of the syllabus. Each day, I made a point of referencing this oversized cardboard elephant that was so prominently hiding behind the cardboard panel at the front of the classroom, hammering home the idea that we as a class would be working together to solve this secret mission. I reminded them that it was up to students to bring their very best to make sure that we were prepared for whatever.

At the end of the first week, I removed the cardboard to reveal the mission:

BIG GOAL: EVERYONE*
will pass the HSA exam on their first try!
(*Yes, everyone. That means YOU!)

The mission was clear. And because we'd made such a ridiculously big deal of building the hype and suspense surrounding the TOP SECRET goal before we'd even set it in action, students were hooked from jump street. Aristotle reminded us that "all men by nature desire to know." It's human nature to want the things that we can't have. And so, with the big reveal in the bag, we set out to achieve the impossible together.

Full disclosure: We fell just short of that goal. A handful of my students ultimately didn't pass the standardized state exam on their first try that year. And although the task lived up to its *Mission: Impossible* reputation, my students ended up with the highest HSA scores in our entire building. So yeah, we didn't quite hit our target. But it was hard not to be proud of every single one of the students when my admin team later informed me that my classes also achieved the second-highest HSA pass rate that year from *all schools in the entire county* and *across all tested subjects*.

And it all started with a *free*, flimsy old piece of cardboard!

You and Your Five Senses

The crisp, sugary smell of fresh-baked sweets wafting through the streets from the confectionery on Main Street, USA. The fruity splash of pineapple Dole Whips enjoyed in the hot sun of Adventureland. The savory sizzle of jumbo-sized turkey legs so darn big that people swear they're actually made of emu . . . Disney theme parks are truly a feast for all five senses.

Walt Disney himself was a perpetual believer in what he called "plussing it"—using added layers of theme and detail to continue enriching the experience even after it was more than impressive enough to answer his harshest critics. I'll let him explain:

"The park means a lot to me in that it's something that will never be finished. Something that I can keep developing, keep plussing and adding to—it's alive. It will be a live, breathing thing that will need changes."

Let's take the idea of theming one step further and brainstorm ideas on how we can create a multisensory classroom—how we can "plus it."

Sight

Close your eyes and imagine the sight of a Disney theme park at night. Can you picture an iconic castle towering high as a dazzling display of fireworks explodes in a sea of glittering brilliance, throwing light and color everywhere the eye can see?

Now look up!

Your entire classroom is a blank canvas of limitless possibilities for learning. What might happen if you grabbed a few blank sheets of paper and taped essential questions for each new unit directly to your ceiling? Your essential questions would then, quite literally, hang over your head like fireworks throughout a full year of study. Hanging these questions also makes them a natural point of reference, helping students connect their daily activity with the bigger picture of why they're even studying any of this stuff in the first place.

You might also consider playing with the colors of the classroom itself. Dust off some old lamps from IKEA to instantly transform any classroom into a groovy "poetry cafe." Or grab a Lava Lamp in the color that best fits your unit (or one of those cheap knockoffs with the swirly sparkles inside) and position it prominently in a place where everyone can see it. Suddenly you're not just studying the solar system or the oceans but welcoming your students to Mission Control in the farthest reaches of outer space or the deepest depths of SeaBase 3000. Captivate your students' imaginations, and there will be no limit to what they can achieve.

Touch

When my students were studying Charles Dickens's *A Christmas Carol*, we met Jacob Marley's ghost, weighed down in the afterlife by the heavy chains of regret forged from his time on earth. To really help this character leap off of the page, we started class with an easy warm-up question: "Have you ever done something you've later regretted?" Students wrote their answers on individual slips of paper, which we then stapled together to form one massive paper chain. *Boom!* Not only did we fashion a concrete visual to help hammer home the deeper theme at play, but we kept the physical chain on display throughout the remainder of the unit, offering students a three-dimensional anchor chart that they could literally pick up and hold in their hands.

What artifacts from your content area might lend themselves to a similarly tactile activity?

Sound

Moms and dads might not like to admit it, but there really are fewer things more memorable about a Disney vacation than the timeless refrain of "It's a Small World (After All)." Let's face it, even the corniest of musical scores can transport us to faraway places. Take a cue from the Mouse and really make your classroom sing!

Reading something scary, like a short story from Edgar Allan Poe? Turn off all lights and draw your blinds, so the space is as dark as possible from the moment students set foot in your door. Fire up some mournful orchestral piece like Samuel Barber's "Adagio for Strings" in the background, and the atmosphere will feel darker, heavier, and more ominous instantly. Think of the endless possibilities racing through students' imaginations as they enter your classroom! Then "plus it" by having them write (or read) the warm-up activity, using only the light from their cell phone flashlights to guide the way.

Smell

Psychologists will tell us that the sense of smell is more closely linked to memory than any other sense. Though many schools have strict rules against lighting candles and playing with fire, a little bit of theming can go a long way in playing to the olfactory senses. If you're studying the chemical properties of sulfur, you can lock a rotten egg inside a tightly sealed plastic container for only the bravest of students to explore. If you're reading a story set on an exotic beach, you can use a reed diffuser to disperse the sweet smell of citrus blossoms. And on a crisp fall day, even math classes can get in on the multisensory action by letting students step outside into the fresh air to examine angles while tracing geometric patterns in a pile of fallen leaves.

Taste

There's a lot more to tickling a kid's taste buds than throwing random pizza parties in your classroom. Reading a holiday classic? Consider serving paper cups of cider or hot cocoa with mini marshmallows. A science class studying caverns? Hello, rock candy! Or transform a social studies lesson from the 1800s into a virtual class trip with some root beer and sarsaparilla to turn your classroom into a G-rated Wild West saloon.

Walt Disney once said, "Around here we don't look backwards for very long. We keep moving forward, opening up new doors and doing new things because we're curious . . . and curiosity keeps leading us down new paths." The exact same thing can and should be said for the attitude and hunger that we bring to our teaching practices. Yes, the cost of these "plussing" endeavors can certainly add up over time, but they demand more effort than money. Enthusiasm is infectious, and our students notice when we go the extra mile on their behalf. No matter how you approach your practice, teaching demands an incredible amount of work. Would you rather . . .

Put in the time creating, engaging, and inspiring?

or

Put in the time managing, correcting, and punishing?

Spoiler: Kids learn more from grown-ups they like. And I didn't get into teaching to be the bad guy.

One Little Spark

I love these flights of fancy. Searching the universe for sounds, colors, ideas, anything that sparks the imagination. A sun beam, that's a good one. Ho, ho, hooo. Everything I collect can inspire amazing and marvelous new ideas, and you never know what kind of figment you may come up with.

—The Dreamfinder, "The Journey into Imagination" Ride

Okay, so we've mastered the art of spooky songs for short stories and hot cocoa for Christmas. But as the lyrics from Disney's "One Little Spark" remind us, sometimes even the tiniest spark of imagination can really take on an entire world of its own. Now that you've nailed down the basics of classroom theming, let's kick this #EDrenaline rush into high speed!

Here's the unlikely story of how a missing sheet of chart paper ended up being the one little spark that turned a barnyard allegory into a lesson that students would never forget.

The One Little Spark

It was my second year of teaching in a high-needs, urban, high school just outside of Washington, D.C. Teacher turnover rates were high, HSA scores were failing, and daily suspension rates regularly numbered in the dozens as classroom behavior issues and hallway fights were an everyday occurrence. I had six jam-packed class sections of thirty-plus tenth graders. Most students were reading four or more years below grade level, and we were starting a unit on George Orwell's *Animal Farm*.

It was a tough sell.

Stuck for alternatives, my thought was to grab a big old sheet of white paper and make an anchor chart with the Seven Commandments that the pigs dream up upon starting their barn-yard revolution. Then, as the unit progressed, I would replace this chart with a revised one every few days, adjusting the rules ever so slightly as we went to reflect the pigs' increasingly power-hungry agenda.

I headed down to the teacher workroom to grab my supplies. Even though our school was hurting for funds, one of the resources we had in pretty regular supply was giant reams of butcher paper in a bunch of different colors. Teachers typically used them to create backgrounds for their bulletin boards. The only problem was that since I was teaching this unit in November, most of the butcher paper had been pretty well picked over, leaving me little to choose from except for giant sheets of muddy brown, dark red, and a dusky, sun-bleached yellow. All of these rolls had clearly seen better days, and it was immediately apparent that none of them would be useful for posting a class anchor chart with any legible writing, especially if I was hoping to make any stealthy changes to it as the unit progressed.

Ugh.

So I thought. *Ugly brown. Dark red. And sun-bleached yellow.* Hardly the stuff of classroom inspiration. How in the world was this supposed to get my students even remotely interested in a thinly veiled allegory about the rise of Soviet Russia?

And that's when it hit me.

The Heart of All Creation

I grabbed a bit of the yellow and as much of the red butcher paper as I could carry, and I raced back to my classroom to begin work creating some giant crimson and gold Soviet flags to hang in my room.

About now is the part where I should tell you that I was fully aware that peddling communist pig propaganda onto a room full of impressionable sixteen-year-olds was pushing the envelope and probably not the best way to ingratiate myself to my school administrators. But every reliable metric and benchmark exam was practically screaming at us that our traditional approaches just weren't working. So I spent the next few hours draping two giant banners from ceiling to floor on either side of my projection screen and adorning them with the iconic hammer and sickle icon set against a blood-red background.

Now picture this scene: Here I am, a white, second-year teacher in a high-needs, urban, high school, decorating my classroom with massive displays of Soviet propaganda at about seven o'clock on a Friday night, when the school security officer, an African American policeman in full uniform, showed up at my door. I thought for sure that I was headed for the unemployment line at best, or at worst, a Siberian prison camp.

Here's the conversation as I remember it:

Officer: "What is all this?"

Me (stammering): "It . . . it . . . it's for a book I'm teaching next week, officer . . . I . . ."

Officer (stepping closer, inspecting the massive twin pillars of twelve-foot class decor): "What book?"

Me (now legitimately terrified): "George Orwell's *Animal Farm*, sir. It's an allegory about Soviet Russia."

Silence. Like, forever.

Me (panicking): "Look, officer. I didn't mean any harm by it. And I'm happy to take everything down if you. . . "

Officer: "Take everything down? Are you kidding? This is fantastic. *Animal Farm* is my favorite book of all time! How can I help you with this?"

After I picked my jaw back up off the floor and checked my heartbeat to make sure I was, in fact, still alive, the officer and I worked together to take the themed classroom transformation to an entirely different level, one beyond even my wildest dreams. We

printed out dozens of sheets of paper with icons of Che Guevara, Martin Luther King, and Mahatma Gandhi. We typed up dozens more themed propaganda-style messages about anything that we could think of, everything from "Obey" to "Down with Big Brother!"

Then we emptied the contents of my desk drawers, flipped my teacher desk on its side, and covered it in a third, red banner to create the illusion of a massive speaker's podium placed dead center between the two, festooned banners.

But the security officer had one last idea in mind that completely blew me out of the water.

The #EDrenaline Rush

The following Monday, students entered the classroom sufficiently shocked at the classroom transformation. They were captivated by the immersive decorations and the theming details, and they immediately started asking all sorts of questions about each of the revolutionary posters on the walls.

"Mr. Meehan, what does this first symbol mean?"

"Who is Big Brother?"

"Why should we 'remember, remember the fifth of November?'"

Mission accomplished. Our unit was off to an outstanding start. For the next four days, we went about trying to peel back the mysterious layers of this radical classroom transformation by reading the first few chapters of *Animal Farm*. All the while, we related the story to the current state of American politics, supplementing our discussion with articles ranging from Occupy Wall Street to conversations about state censorship. Each day, students raised questions regarding freedom of speech, the right to protest, and the price an individual must be willing to pay to speak truth to power in a system designed to oppress its citizens.

That was, until Friday morning . . .

Right on schedule, as I was in mid-sentence denouncing the evils of government oppression, my good friend the security officer arrived at my doorway flanked by our vice principal and two other members of our school administration. Deadpan, the officer said, "Mr. Meehan, we are going to need you to come with us."

And just like that, I was escorted out of the classroom and students were left under the supervision of the vice principal, who looked at all the propaganda with stone-faced bewilderment, as if she were seeing it all for the first time. She shook her head and said, "Oh no. We need to take all of this down right away."

For the longest three minutes of my students' lives, Kathy McCormack expertly played the part of shocked school administrator turned state-sponsored censor. (It helped that she is a U.S. Army veteran and knows how to play it tough.) She refused to answer questions and instructed each student to write down exactly what had happened in the days leading up to her "unscheduled" arrival, so she could make her proper determination on how the school should proceed.

When I returned three minutes later, you could have heard a pin drop. Visibly shaken and on the receiving end of an ice-cold stare from Mrs. McCormack as she exited, I instructed my students to just keep writing as I began tearing the propaganda posters off the walls around them in a sullen display of defeat.

One by one, the posters came down, shaking my head as I made my way around the walls to the farthest corner of the classroom . . . where I casually reached to the topmost corner of a bookcase and pulled out a hidden video camera, which had been filming the entire process from the first bell of class.

Immediately, the students realized that their mild-mannered English teacher was safe from the authorities, and this entire ordeal was the finishing touch on an elaborate teaching stunt that we'd worked together to orchestrate all along. The class went wild with glee.

Not only that, but they swore each other to secrecy and promised not to tell the other class sections, so we could repeat the same social experiment not one, not two, not three, not four, but *five* additional times over the next forty-eight hours. And to give my students all the credit they deserve, keeping a secret between high school class sections is already a minor miracle when the stakes are something as easily shared as the answers to a multiple-choice test. But something like this? Earning their trust and secrecy was a thing of legend, and I am so thankful for their willingness to play ball.

And it all started with one little spark.

Aside from helping my students learn the content of the unit, this comprehensive, multi-layered theming truly made them realize that their teachers, their curriculum, their school security, and their administration were a united force for their best interests. On that day—even if only for a few brief moments—we ceased being mere "teachers," "security guards," "students," and "administrators." Instead, we came together as cooperative learners on a common journey, bound together by mutual admiration, imagination, and respect. While the activity was extreme, it helped students see just how far I was willing to go on their behalf, and they immediately extended me their full confidence in return. My classes each went on to have the highest HSA scores in the building, and I didn't write a single detention all year.

That's the game-changing power of an #EDrenaline rush.

Questions for Discussion

1 . What is the story of your classroom? How might your curriculum lend itself to a clearly divisible, unit-by-unit, pacing guide with differently themed "lands" to clarify the edges between them?

2. How might multi-sensory theming "plus" a lesson that's already a part of your curriculum? How might future tense verbs smell? What could geometry taste like?

3. Disney Imagineers call early brainstorming sessions the "blue sky phase"—and there are no wrong answers here. What would your favorite unit look like if money was no object and the Disney corporation decided to transform it into a full-blown theme park?

Chapter 2

Weenies, Wait Times, and Talking Walls

Those things you learn without joy you will forget easily.

—Old Finnish Saying

P icture this: You're three days into a weeklong vacation at your favorite theme park. It should be an amazing escape from reality, but between the heat, the lines, the prices, the crowds, and all that time spent walking for hours on end, the kids are getting cranky, and the pixie dust is starting to wear off.

It's time for weenies, wait times, and talking walls.

Weenies

While your local boardwalk's Ferris wheel or county fair's bumper cars might not have trouble matching the fun factor of many of the Disney attractions, they typically fall short of the "Disney Magic" due to all the time you spend waiting for the ride. Losing momentum can really disrupt your "flow" state and pull you out of even the most exciting of vacations. As Tom Petty once sang, "the waiting is the hardest part." And so even the most gung-ho of vacationers can tell you that it's vital to maintain momentum while waiting in line, since it's pretty much the single activity that you'll be doing for the majority of your day at most every amusement park on the planet.

That's why at the Disney parks, waiting in line is just as much a part of the ride as the actual seated portion of the attraction itself.

Take the Haunted Mansion: You start by walking in a slow funeral march up to a spooky house on a hill, passing a horseless hearse carriage, coiling through an overgrown graveyard, and entering the doors of a Victorian manor where a sour-faced servant dressed in dark green and black greets you. With a frown, you are quickly ushered into a parlor waiting room full of strangers and instructed to stand in the "dead center" of the room before the doors snap shut and this haunted corridor appears to stretch before your very eyes.

You're not even on the ride yet! Behold, the power of the weenies.

Borrowing from his experience working in film and television, Walt Disney was a big believer in using oversized visual aids to draw an audience's attention to specific items and things to look for. Walt called these world-building tools "weenies"—named after the hot dog treats that were often used on Hollywood movie sets to get canine actors to perform on cue. All of those spooky props outside of The Haunted Mansion? Weenies. They don't really *do* anything, per se. But they are ridiculously effective at distracting you from the insufferable wait times.

That's why Disney calls everything an "attraction" or an "experience." Rides are only a small part of the fun.

Now compare this with the traditional system of education, where students spend the majority of their academic lives in an endless parade of compliance, drudgery, and this unshakable feeling that they're really no more than another nameless face in the crowd. And when they get to the end of the line, they're rewarded not with a fancy roller coaster but with a test. When adrenaline levels are low, it's no surprise that students are snoozing their afternoons away. But can every single class be an action-packed thrill ride? Absolutely! Waiting is part of the game. That's why we need some classroom weenies, stat!

Weenies are storytelling props that make a space come to life. And in the classroom, it's not just a case of semi-regular displays of student work: This is all about metacognition. The only thing more powerful than ownership is authorship. A classroom's walls belong to the learners inside just as much as they do to the teacher. That's why it's critically important that these same students have a say in what is helping to shape the physical space that surrounds them. Every single time a new addition is made to the classroom decor, students should have had a hand in its making or an understanding of its creation. They can use this information as a springboard to help spark curiosity for the adventure that is to come.

Flat Stanley

Studying anatomy? Have students break into teams and trace the outline of the human body on day one of a new unit. Then have them revisit their full-sized tracings to keep adding in new anatomical details, organs, and systems as your course explores all the complex functions of the human body throughout the year. Let the anchor chart grow and evolve as students learn more information.

This same activity is a great way to bring life and energy to classes outside of the sciences! Students can break into teams to create "living" anchor charts in which they trace their outlines. The outlines can serve as major historical figures or literary characters. Revisit the chart again and again throughout your unit to continue adding historical details (like George Washington's famed "wooden" teeth) as well as important symbols (like the apocryphal, cherry tree-chopping axe) and metaphorical connections to illustrate major themes in the unit (like having the "heart of a lion" or the "guts" to decline the offer to become America's king).

Timeless Timelines

We've all seen a math class with a bulletin board-like border that keeps track of all the digits that can fit in the space from the number Pi (starting always with the familiar 3.14). But could students do the same for a living history timeline? Let's say your social studies class started with 1776. Work with teammates to keep adding new panels to your timeline as each unit progresses. Timelines that grow, morph, and evolve are superpowered tools students can use to reflect on their own thinking. What's "wall worthy?" What can we leave behind?

Periodic Table Pokémon

Stanford-educated researcher turned Arizona State University professor of literacy studies James Paul Gee once said that Pokémon might just be the single best literacy program ever devised. Greg Toppo, senior editor of *Inside Higher Ed* and author of *The Game Believes in You: How Digital Play Can Make Our Kids Smarter*, wrote,

> While educators debated whether children learn to read best through drill-and-practice phonics or 'whole language' instruction, Nintendo was, quite informally, teaching a generation of children how to read. Pokémon also taught children how to analyze and classify more than 700 different types of creatures through trading cards that were dense with specialized, technical, cross-referenced text.

Think about it: There is no such thing as a "Pokémon Achievement Gap." Ask any kid in the country—black or white, rich or poor, male or female—and chances are really good that they will be able to tell you TONS of incredibly detailed information about Pokémon. Types, abilities, evolutionary history, you

31

name it. But ask these same kids to explain even a dozen elements on the periodic table, and immediately it's like you're staring at a Snorlax. It's not that our children can't learn. It's that we haven't found the right way to speak to them to make them want to.

So could you supercharge a rote taxonomy memorization activity by taking a cue from Pokémon?

Here's one way:

Divide students up into teams and assign them one specific element (or a handful) at a time. Then ask them to re-envision these same elements as if they were Pokémon-like monsters. What would the Carbon Pokémon look like? What special powers would it have? Which monsters is it most likely to befriend? To challenge?

Suddenly, you've transformed your periodic table into a year-long "monster battle." Students will design new creatures as they

encounter new elements, each time offering visuals and written supports of their rationales for each selection. By the end of the school year, your Periodic Table has become a student-centered Pokémon Hall of Fame. And the best part is that your students are the ones fueling the creative energy.

Magic Mirror on the Wall

In February of 2012, Walt Disney World debuted the Sorcerers of the Magic Kingdom game, an interactive scavenger hunt where "apprentices" could visit special locations hidden all throughout the park to help Merlin battle a bevy of familiar Disney baddies by scanning collectible cards and revealing secret quests with inter-active video animations. But of course, they could, right? I mean, Disney is worth somewhere in the neighborhood of $150 billion. That sort of next-generation, interactive, video technology cer-tainly doesn't come cheap.

Well, it does now.

Augmented Reality (AR) apps have improved by leaps and bounds since 2012. And today, free apps like HP Reveal (formerly Aurasma), Blippar, and Metaverse give you the ability to create and share interactive scannables right from your smartphone, hiding an entire invisible universe of embedded video or text in plain sight. And if you're scared of AR? A simple QR code can do the trick just as well. Suddenly that Watson and Crick photo becomes a three-dimensional model of the double helix. That image of Shakespeare's Globe Theatre becomes a video rendition of *Hamlet's* "to be or not to be." And that timeline of the Civil War transforms into a live reenactment of Lincoln's Gettysburg Address.

What fun could your students have in a scavenger hunt for invisible secrets?

Facebook Walls

Interactive anchor charts can help students keep track of individual character behaviors throughout a long-form unit of study. They are especially helpful when studying longer works, like the plays of Shakespeare, but these bad boys can be adapted to any grade level with a few oversized sheets of chart paper, a quick social media skin, and a TON of sticky notes.

For our study of *Julius Caesar*, we created oversized Facebook-inspired anchor charts for each of the major characters in the play. To pre-teach character relationships, I picked a handful of characters from the SpongeBob SquarePants universe to help students get a feel for how all these individuals were connected. (SpongeBob was Julius Caesar, his best friend, Patrick, was Brutus, and his grouchy neighbor, Squidward, was Casca.)

Note that the setup for each anchor chart is very minimal. Write the word "Facebook" on an oversized sheet of paper, provide the character's profile photo (or have students draw one!), and add a small box in the lower left-hand corner to list basic character information as you encounter it (e.g., relationships, relatives, hometown, etc.). Everything else is completely blank at the start of

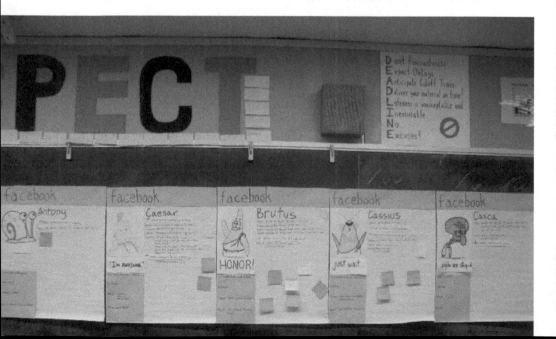

the unit because students will be building these anchor charts and adding to them as the unit progresses.

Each day as we read, students kept track of character behaviors and submitted "status updates," using Post-It notes for warm-ups, share-outs, and exit ticket activities. After we discussed each status update as a class, we'd take the most relevant of them and transfer them in magic marker as permanent additions to the character's wall.

The day-to-day unit activity pretty much runs itself. Just pass out a stack of sticky notes to each student and stop at regular intervals to solicit prompt questions for possible character-specific status updates. Here are some ideas:

- **Characterization:** Based on the behavior that we just witnessed from the text, what type of person is [character x]? If they had to pick a favorite type of music / movie / TV show—what might they be listening to or watching right now? Jot it down on a sticky note, then post it on that character's wall.

- **Character Relationships:** What do you think [character x] might say to [character y] if they had Facebook (or Twitter, etc.) right now? Write it on a sticky note from the perspective of [character x] and then go post it on that other character's wall.

- **Symbolism:** If [character x] was using Instagram, what photo might they share at this moment? Why? Doodle it on your sticky note and write a quick caption. Then post it on that character's wall.

- **Foreshadowing:** Is [character x] the type of person who sees what's coming or has a plan for something that might happen in the future? Let's give them a status update! Write something that they might be looking forward to (or dreading) and post it on their wall.

- **Historical Connections:** Let's take a moment to share a video on [character x]'s wall that might help them make sense of their current dilemma/predicament. Pull up YouTube on your devices and find a short video that will help them see into the future and make sense of how this particular period in history plays out. You'll want to accompany your post with a quick explanation of why, exactly, they should watch this video.

Word Clouds

Interactive word walls are outstanding and immersive tools to introduce students to key terms, characters, and vocabulary before, during, and after a new unit of study. More than just a gorgeous piece of classroom wall décor, these suckers are an invaluable pre-teaching and re-teaching resource to help students make meaning of new units as their stories unfold.

Double the bang for your buck with a word cloud by letting the students help make the anchor chart image themselves! On day one of your unit, start your class by projecting your chosen shape onto sheets of white chart paper and asking students to trace each of the words that it contains. Then let them brainstorm and make predictions about where they think the unit might be headed.

The image on the previous page shows a word cloud of the most frequently occurring words in Shakespeare's *Julius Caesar* as if the entire play were a giant bomb. Judging from the size of the character names that the "bomb" contains, students quickly see which characters will be crucial to setting off the bomb's explosion and begin the play with, and continue to discuss, various conspiracy theories. This served as an *awesome* pre-teaching resource. It heightened the suspense and drama as we revisited the "ticking time bomb" idea throughout the play. The play is named after Julius Caesar, but *Brutus* is clearly the man at the center of all the action. Suddenly, Caesar's famous "*Et tu, Brute?*" line really does feel like an explosion through the heart.

Dead Word Graveyard

If there's a particular word or phrase that you're tired of hearing in your classroom, consider writing it on a simple sheet of white paper and adding it to the "Dead Word Graveyard" at a far end of your classroom, perhaps while including a more school-appropriate suggestion as the word's "epitaph" just underneath its title. You might even consider taking a few moments to invite students to pay their respects in a quick mock funeral as the word is laid to its final rest, never again to be heard in your classroom.

In 2010, "Shut up" died in my classroom and was replaced with "Please be quiet." It was a terrible tragedy, and it will be missed. In 2015, we bid farewell to "bae," which was lost in a horrible accident and taken long before its time. These days, I've got a countdown on "That's lit, bro!" which may well have been taken off of life support by the time that this book reaches print.

Students. Eat. This. Up.

Wait Times

Whether you're adding dead words to a graveyard or making educated guesses inspired by massive word clouds, weenies really help the hours fly right by on the days when momentum might otherwise be lost. But even for the most experienced theme park junkies, unexpected wait times can be a total buzzkill, so let's take a closer look at one last Disney trick to help alleviate the logjam of those unavoidable queues in the classroom. When done right, the inevitable moments where you're "just passing the time" can really help students have the time of their lives.

No Red Lights in Disney World

In a 2015 *Wired* article titled "Disney's $1 Billion Bet on a Magical Wristband," Cliff Kuang explains how the folks at the Disney Parks recently overhauled their entire guest experience by pouring a crazy amount of cash into developing the Magic Band, a wearable technology infrastructure that serves as everything from a park pass to an electronic ride queueing system to a hotel room key. The article cites Meg Crofton, then president of Walt Disney World Resort, whose team set out to streamline guests' enjoyment of the Disney World experience, saying, "We were looking for pain points. What are the barriers to getting into the experience faster?"

Say hello to the Magic Band.

Thanks to special scanners located at entrance turnstiles, ride queues, and retail counters throughout Walt Disney World, guests now have the power to walk right in to their next experience with the wave of their arm while their wearable wristband "magically" keeps track of everything, including credit card information, pre-scheduled ride passes, and dining reservations. Kuang explains, "When everything works, the reader flashes green and emits a pleasing tone; if something goes wrong, it glows blue—never red. Red lights are forbidden at Disney, as they imply something bad happened. Nothing bad can happen at Disney World."

Swap out the words "guest experience" for "graded student work," and you've got one of the biggest pain points in all of teaching—the sheer amount of time it takes to return graded work! But what if you could make returning papers as easy as a wave of your magical teacher hand, ditching the traditional red pen in favor of a more pleasing system of real-time feedback that's as friendly as a blue light reminder that there is still some room for improvement?

	KEYWORD INQUIRY LOG		RESEARCH JOURNALS		TEACHER CONFERENCE		STUDENT NAME
	☐ GREAT ☐ GOOD ☐ OK		☐ GREAT ☐ GOOD ☐ OK		☐ GREAT ☐ GOOD ☐ OK		
	TOPIC		THESIS		3 SPORTS		**TEXT FOR RESEARCH**
	☐ GREAT ☐ GOOD ☐ OK		☐ GREAT ☐ GOOD ☐ OK		☐ GREAT ☐ GOOD ☐ OK		
	BRAINSTORM		WORKS CITED		OUTLINE		(GREAT x 10)
	☐ GREAT ☐ GOOD ☐ OK		☐ GREAT ☐ GOOD ☐ OK		☐ GREAT ☐ GOOD ☐ OK		+
	ROUGH DRAFT		PEER REVIEW		INDEPENDENT WRITING		(GOOD x 5)
	☐ GREAT ☐ GOOD ☐ OK		☐ GREAT ☐ GOOD ☐ OK		☐ GREAT ☐ GOOD ☐ OK		**FINAL SCORE**

Snag a fully editable copy of the No Red Lights
rubric at EDrenalineRush.com/Resources.

Bippidi boppidi *BOOM!* That's why I dreamed up the "No Red Lights" rubric, quite possibly one of my all-time favorite Disney-inspired classroom creations. The idea is simple: Students (or teams) work at their own pace to complete checkpoint stages of a larger work product. And each time they're ready to make their way through a new checkpoint (just like a park guest moving freely about a theme park en route to a new ride), they're able to get magical on-the-spot teacher feedback simply by raising their hands. These checkpoint stages are typically super short, like forming a well-constructed thesis statement, solving the first steps of a much longer mathematical equation, or drafting a proper transition sentence between two paragraphs. The magic of the checkpoint is that when the student calls the teacher over to spot-check their work as soon as they've made their way through the assigned task, the teacher is able to give a quick look at their work product and offer them real-time feedback as to whether or not their submission is "Great," "Good," or only just "Okay."

No red lights.

The old-school approach—amusement park turnstiles and cash registers—created bottlenecks at park entry and checkout counters as visitors fumbled with paper tickets, credit cards, and coins. Similarly, the traditional approach to work product checkpoints in classrooms mandates that every student submit the same work product on the same day, at which point it is up to the teacher to score all submissions at once while papers invariably stack up on desks awaiting the red pen.

"No Red Lights" rubrics are nothing like the endless note card stacks or the bottomless essay piles of yesteryear. Instead of collecting everything from every student at once and then grading every submission for every possible mistake at the same time, the teacher can provide each student a super-speedy thirty-second review at strategic checkpoints along their self-paced journey, along with some friendly on-the-spot feedback to help learners see what's working and where there's still a bit of work to be done. And just like a theme park visit, kids always have the option to hop back to a particular attraction after giving it a ride for the first time.

Since the work product is either "Great," "Good," or "Okay," there are never any logjams for student learning. If a student gets a "Great" work product, they can move to the next checkpoint with confidence, and the teacher can encourage them to really stretch their learning at the next station as they make their way forward at their own pace. If the work product is "Good," a teacher can provide a thirty-second pep-talk to help the student see where there's still a bit of finessing to be done (again, no red lights in Disney!)— which will inevitably help steer the learner back toward a stronger submission on the way to the next checkpoint. And if the bite-sized work product is only "Okay," teacher and student can discuss where the submission falls short. The teacher can offer on-the-spot feedback as appropriate and encourage the student to make necessary tweaks as needed before re-submitting at the same checkpoint in order to sail forward again with confidence that there's nothing but green lights ahead!

Put Our Service to the Test

Of course, no trip to a Disney theme park would be complete without a quick customer satisfaction survey! In the early days of Disneyland, Walt Disney himself would famously stroll down Main Street USA talking with park guests, peppering them with questions about their time in the park, and listening intently to what they had to say. To this day, the Disney parks' fanatical attention to detail is a thing of legend, and if you hang out just inside of the park entrance, you'll often spot a friendly employee armed with a tablet and a few short questions asking for guest feedback. If you're likewise in the market to enhance the "guest" experience in your classroom, consider providing regular opportunities for students to offer feedback on their learning and your instructional design as they complete each unit with something as simple as a short survey in a Google Form. Which activities worked? Which attractions are showing their age or could use a "new coat of paint?" Where can you take a cue from student feedback and "plus it" in your pedagogy?

Questions for Discussion

1. If you have your own classroom, think of a unit that you currently teach that lends itself to a "weenie." What materials would you need to create an eye-catching visual that could spark student interest and inspire deeper engagement?

2. Think of a unit in your curriculum that could be presented as a word cloud or a Pokémon-style taxonomy. What shape or creatures could you select for this particular content and why? How might a themed anchor chart enhance student interaction with your course content?

3. Consider the possibilities of a "No Red Lights" rubric activity in your classroom. Is there a particular lesson that could be enhanced if it were broken into smaller work product checkpoints with a similar "Great," "Good," and "Okay" approach with real-time feedback?

Chapter 3

Exit Through
The Gift Shop

*Look at this. It's worthless—ten dollars from
a vendor in the street. But I take it, I bury
it in the sand for a thousand years,
and it becomes priceless.*

—René Belloq, *Raiders of the Lost Ark*

There's a running joke among the Disney faithful that "every ride ends with a gift shop." It might not be the subtlest way to squeeze a few extra dollars out of happy tourist families, but it certainly is among the most effective. As Jason Howse (@MrHExperience), a teacher friend from Regina, Saskatchewan, Canada, once pointed out to me, students have such a strong sense of belonging to the fantasy world of a theme park that they genuinely feel the need to own a piece of it.

But can the same be said for our classrooms? Do our students feel this sense of connection to the space they spend the majority of their days in?

Drawing inspiration from theme-park-inspired odds and ends ranging from overstuffed teddy bears to Mickey Mouse balloons and the classic carnival midway games of yesteryear, I've packed this chapter with mini games and tangible ways to liven up any classroom with hands-on learning. Think of it as a gift shop of pedagogical souvenirs designed to leave your learners wanting more!

Content Bracketology

- **An #EDrenaline Rush Alternative to:** Traditional essay tests or in-class debates

- **Feels Just Like:** Cheering for your heroes alongside a parade route

Off to Work We Go

Use your course content to fill in all the "teams" in head-to-head matchups for the first round of a giant tournament bracket, then pose a totally subjective question like, "Which of these teams is the strongest?" (or "the bravest" or "the best", etc.). When my classes review American literature, we put 64 characters in a head-to-head "March Sadness" showdown, where student votes determine which character is most deserving of our empathy. Print one copy of these tournament brackets for each student in your class and have students fill in their winners for ALL rounds of the tournament before opening discussion to the floor for an "Apples to Apples"-style debate where students offer arguments as to why a particular "team" should be declared the winner in the slated, head-to-head matchups.

Set an overhead timer to use as a shot clock for each timed round of play and conclude each matchup with a class-wide vote. This is an outstanding way to spark nonlinear thinking and critical listening skills. The fact that many students' brackets will inevitably get busted in early rounds of play rewards creative problem solving and strategic approaches to rhetorical appeals. As players dig deep to develop alternate arguments in subsequent rounds, they hope to topple the still-intact brackets of their classmates.

Spinner Games

- **An #EDrenaline Rush Alternative To:** Any traditional assignment with multiple prompt questions

- **Feels Just Like:** Winning a giant stuffed animal from an oversized wheel of chance

Off to Work We Go

Take a traditional assignment with numbered questions and put each question on a strip of paper. Set a timer on the board and inform the class that everyone will need to answer (x) questions before time expires. Then have students spin an electronic wheel to select a numbered prompt question as determined by their very own oversized boardwalk-style wheel of chance. Keep the energy high as students spin, solve, and repeat until time expires. This can be done individually or in teams.

Tip: Download a spinner app or create a free spinner wheel on Flippity.net.

Don't Break the Ice

- **An #EDrenaline Rush Alternative To:** Group readings where all teams are expected to review the same assigned text or document specific items of information

- **Feels Just Like:** The classic midway game of Whac-a-Mole

Off to Work We Go

Break students into four teams. Assign each team a common text for study. All students should work with their teammates to find as many examples of a certain sort of item in the text as they can before time expires. (Examples include specific poetic techniques, certain conjugations of a verb, prime numbers, etc.) Set a timer and have teams chart their findings on a blank sheet of paper. When time expires, student teams share their findings, *Scattergories*-style,

where individual teams cross out any line-item discoveries that likewise appear in the findings of competing teams.

Use the total number of findings per team to determine the team gameplay turn order for the game, *Don't Break the Ice*. The team with the greatest number of findings plays first, and the team with the lowest number of findings receives the fourth turn in the sequence.

Place four LEGO minifigures onto the *Don't Break the Ice* board game and have one representative from each of the four teams take turns trying to "sink" the minifigures of their foes without accidentally sinking their own minifigure in the process. Players are eliminated once their minifigure is sunk. The team with the last remaining minifigure on the game board is declared the winner for that round. Reset the board and the clock between rounds and have teams repeat the process, scanning the assigned texts for the next "look for" items.

#Hashtag Hunt

- **An #EDrenaline Rush Alternative To:** Low energy annotation assignments

- **Feels Just Like:** Competing with your friends to see who can ride the most rides in a single day

Off to Work We Go

A #Hashtag Hunt is one of my favorite ways to get students fired up about typically low-energy activities like textual annotation. The best part is? It doesn't even require any fancy technology. All you'll need is about a half dozen clear plastic page protectors and a few sticky notes.

To set up your #Hashtag Hunt, label each blank sheet of paper with a different look-for item for each of the six available plastic sleeves. Each plastic sleeve now represents a different choice "station" with its own look-for item for the day. (When I teach *The Great Gatsby*, for example, one station might ask students to make notes of examples of color imagery, while a second asks them to look for signs of deception, and so on.) Set an overhead timer and divide students into four even teams. Ask one representative from each team to approach the board to select one look-for item apiece. (I always like offering two more stations than I have teams, so even the last team to select has some degree of choice.) Start the countdown and challenge each group to annotate with their teammates, using a single blank sheet of paper per team to make note of as many examples of their selected item as they can possibly find (including page numbers!) from the assigned text before time expires. The team with the most findings when time expires wins!

To add an element of surprise to your #Hashtag Hunt, consider using the reverse side of a few of those same plastic page protectors to stash a handful of strategically placed sticky note "wild cards" with freebie bonus points or hidden penalties to keep the game interesting. Maybe a certain station comes pre-loaded with a sticky note awarding +5 extra points (because that station was slightly harder than the others), while another station comes boobytrapped with a -2 point deduction (because you're expecting it to be an easier challenge). When a team starts the game with a surprise deficit, they'll get a sneaking sense that they've stumbled onto an "easier" center—and work *that much harder* as a result. And if a team gets a few points boost to start the hunt? They'll sail into the timed search with a much-needed sense of confidence and momentum to help get them started off on the right foot.

Tip: For a closer look at #Hashtag Hunts, visit EdrenalineRush.com/Resources.

Hungry Hidden Mickeys

- **An #EDrenaline Rush Alternative To:** Activities where students or teams answer large problem sets or identify numerous examples of a specific technique

- **Feels Just Like:** Looking for "Hidden Mickeys" in Disney theme parks

Off to Work We Go

One of the most rewarding experiences for eagle-eyed visitors to the Disney parks is to be on the lookout for so-called "Hidden Mickeys," camouflaged clusters of three circles which create a silhouette of the iconic character. They're cleverly embedded amid the atmospheric theming in rides and attractions throughout the Disney parks. Even though they're hidden in plain sight, Hidden Mickeys can be super tough to spot! Bringing the same activity into your classroom can be just as much fun.

Break students into four teams. Set a timer for five minutes and task groups to work with their teammates to solve multiple problems in a question set (like square roots, basic multiplication tables, or look-for items of a specific literary or poetic technique in an assigned passage).

When the timer expires, complete a lightning-fast recap of each group's answers, comparing answers via student share-out between groups, and award the top-finishing group the highest amount of time possible to play a quick game of *Hungry Hungry Hippos* (say, thirty seconds) and grab as many marbles as they can. Award a short delay to the second-place group (so they join the game five seconds later), with the third-place finisher starting five seconds thereafter and the group with the lowest total of correct items joining the game a full 15 seconds after the first team started mashing the physical *Hungry Hungry Hippos* board game.

Keep a tally of the marbles collected by each group and reset the activity for the next round.

Jenga

- **An #EDrenaline Rush Alternative To:** Typical "hunt and find" review activities

- **Feels Just Like:** Discovering hidden "secrets" in your favorite theme park

Off to Work We Go

The Sorcerers of the Magic Kingdom theme park scavenger hunt activity uses interactive kiosks to reward eagle-eyed travelers with exciting discoveries. While classroom teachers might not have the power to transform a simple review game into a multi-million-dollar augmented reality challenge, you can absolutely capture the same sense of exploration and excitement with a magic marker and a simple stack of building blocks.

Use a marker to mark the top middle portion of each of the fifty-four Jenga blocks with a number from one to fifty-four. (This part is covered when the blocks are stacked together.) Then cook up a list of fifty-four question prompts or look-for items that align with your content area. Set an overhead timer for the total amount of time you'd like to allot to this activity. The goal for each student (or team) is to collect the maximum number of Jenga blocks possible without toppling the Jenga tower. Divide students into teams to begin the game.

Tip: If you're looking to add a technological twist of hidden interaction to your Jenga tower review game, create a series of questions as individual rows in a Google Sheets spreadsheet and install the QR Code Generator add-on. This will automatically turn each question into a QR code. Print out your newly created QR code labels and stick them onto each of the blocks in your game, and students can then take the block back to their group and use a device to scan the code to discover the hidden question prompt that it contains.

Teams can now take turns drawing Jenga blocks one at a time and then working with their teammates to solve the corresponding question that they have selected. Each time a team solves a numbered Jenga block, they can call the teacher over to review it, score a point, and race back to the tower to select a new question. But any student who topples the Jenga tower will automatically lose all of the points that their group had earned up until the tower fell.

LEGO Theme Park Creator

- **An #EDrenaline Rush Alternative To:** Any traditional note-taking activity

- **Feels Just Like:** Designing your very own theme park, a la *Roller Coaster Tycoon*

Off to Work We Go

Divide students into teams of no more than five or six. Set an overhead timer and task teams with creating as many LEGO scenes or set pieces as they can before time expires. Have teams log their findings using Google Slides or a Google Doc—building, photographing, and adding to the electronic document before tearing their construction apart and repeating the process. For a creation to count, it must be grounded in text evidence—which means that groups should always be pairing photographic evidence of their creations with direct lines of textual support. All you'll need is one web-ready device per team!

The Marshmallow Challenge

- **An #EDrenaline Rush Alternative To:** Hokey or canned "team-building" activities

- **Feels Just Like:** Agreeing on a touring plan when everyone wants to go on a different ride at the same time

Off to Work We Go

The Marshmallow Challenge is deceptively simple: Using only dried spaghetti, masking tape, and string, teammates must work together to create the tallest free-standing structure that they can, with the only rule being that a jumbo marshmallow must be placed on top of the tower. The group with the tallest tower still standing at the end of an eighteen-minute time period wins.

This is an excellent way for teachers to model the value of good communication, the importance of working together, and the power of growth mindset.

> **Tip:** To learn more about The Marshmallow Challenge, visit leadershipchallenge.com.

Mr. Potato Head PDSA

- **An #EDrenaline Rush Alternative To:** Traditional lectures about the importance of testing a hypothesis, reviewing data, and distinguishing relevant findings from irrelevant findings

- **Feels Just Like:** Riding a scary roller coaster for the second time in a row

Off to Work We Go

Ever had the urge to jump right back on a super scary roller coaster immediately after you've braved it for the first time? There's a reason kids beg to go on their favorite rides multiple times in a row: Once we've conquered the unknown, we feel bolder, braver, and better prepared the second time around. The Mr. Potato Head "Plan, Design, Study, Act" cycle (PDSA)—also known as the PDCA cycle of "Plan, Design, Check, Act"—is a ridiculously fun activity that blends the finesse of real-time feedback with the rapid adrenaline rush that comes from the opportunity to try, try again.

Tip: For more information, visit ihi.org and search for "Potato Head."

Rock, Paper, Scissors and Thumb War Tournaments

- **An #EDrenaline Rush Alternative To:** Arbitrarily assigning group roles by random numbering

- **Feels Just Like:** Calling "dibs" on the front train car of your favorite roller coaster

Off to Work We Go

Split students into teams of two (for Thumb War) or three (for Rock, Paper, Scissors) and have them square off in hand-to-hand combat to determine the "winner" of the showdown. In a three-person group, the first player to win over BOTH of their teammates is declared the winner. The winners in each group get to assign group roles.

This sort of activity can be used any time the class breaks into group roles. It is an easy way to help students who might not always be the highest-scoring academic performers still feel like they are "winning" in a classroom activity.

Debate Bounce Off

- **An #EDrenaline Rush Alternative To:** Traditional class debates

- **Feels Just Like:** Throwing coins in a fountain

Off to Work We Go

Divide the class in half and assign a different side of an argument to each team. Arrange desks into two facing rows, so opposing teams face one another with a giant galley between them. The goal of the game is to earn ping pong ball shots into a plastic grid frame or bowl as a reward for offering quality arguments in defense of your team's assigned position.

Pose a question to the class to start the debate. Each time a student offers a quality response, slide the plastic grid or bowl somewhere in close proximity to where they are seated and have them take a shot at throwing a ping pong ball into the waiting grid frame located below their desk. If they can land the ball in the grid, they'll pick up a point for their team.

As an added incentive, slide the grid or bowl *that much* closer or further away from a responding student depending on the quality of their response. This encourages higher quality responses, as they will be rewarded with an easier ping pong ball shot while those in need of additional detail might face a more challenging shot.

Rory's Story Cubes

- **An #EDrenaline Rush Alternative To:** Traditional start-of-class quizzes or content recap activities

- **Feels Just Like:** Telling creative stories with larger-than-life characters

Off to Work We Go

Rory's Story Cubes are nine-sided dice with different illustrations on each side. While there are themed sets like "Actions," "Voyages," and "Fantasia," chances are good that most of the images that adorn the nine dice in each set actually have very little to do with your

specific course content. This is perfect for lateral thinking puzzles! Give students different story cube sets to play with. Have them roll the dice to reveal an image (or a series of images) at random. Now have them explain what they've learned from the current unit by creating a series of metaphors in which they successfully incorporate each of the images they've rolled.

Example: Emily Dickinson's life was like a [**fire breathing dragon**] guarding a [**castle tower**] because she had [**shooting star**] incredible poetic talent, but she kept it locked away from the world and lived most of her life as a recluse.

"E Ticket" Investments

- **An #EDrenaline Rush Alternative To:** Traditional sit-and-listen activities during peer presentations

- **Feels Just Like:** Saving up amusement park tickets for Skee-Ball prizes or "E Ticket" rides

Off to Work We Go

Fun fact: In 1955, the price of admission to the Disneyland park was a mere $1 for adults and 50 cents for children. Rather than gouging park guests for a lump sum at the entrance gate, Disney opted to sell books of tickets which could be used to gain entry into the various attractions throughout the park—the smaller, less popular rides were designated as 10 cent "A Ticket" attractions, while the 85 cent "E Tickets" were reserved for headline rides like the Pirates of the Caribbean. The theory was that the more popular the attraction, the more folks would be willing to pay to see it.

"E Ticket" investments put a similar twist on a traditional parade of peer presentations. Give each student one raffle ticket apiece and task them with secretly "investing" these tickets in the most promising project after all of their peers have presented.

Think of this like a classroom game of *Shark Tank*—with the goal of awarding and rewarding the strongest "pitches" with award payouts for both the investor *and* the pitch presenter. This reduces the tendency to merely vote for one's friends, as the biggest payout comes from paying closest attention to which presentations are attracting the most buzz from the "guests" in your park!

Text Quest

- **An #EDrenaline Rush Alternative To:** Traditional "gotcha quiz" warm-ups

- **Feels Just Like:** Entering the world of a story in an interactive queue like Disney's Haunted Mansion

Off to Work We Go

Rather than punishing learners with an arbitrary set of five quick question items to see who's read the book, this Role Playing Game-like activity is designed to help teachers draw thematic inspiration from any assigned text while helping students build empathy with the very characters who inhabit this same world. And all you'll need is a set of Role Playing Game dice.

A Text Quest begins by offering a warm-up prompt scenario inspired by the previous night's reading and the chance to make a decision as if they were in a character's shoes. (Example: Maybe Scout Finch has the choice to sneak into Boo Radley's yard or to stand up to her older brother, Jem, and leave her poor reclusive neighbor alone.) Teachers present the "What would you do?" style prompt on the overhead and offer student teams the choice to pursue one of three options ranging from "EASY," "MEDIUM," or "HARD." Student groups of four to five students will be given two to three minutes to dialogue and strategize together as a group, weighing the pros and cons of each decision in an attempt to see

EASY	MEDIUM	HARD
Keep playing along their silly game and it'll pass. Boo Radley is a mystery! And it'd be fun to meet him.	Try to convince Dill to play a different game. Maybe you can roll down the hill in a tire instead of picking on Boo.	Tell Jem to stop bothering your neighbor. Boo Radley never bothered you, and he just wants to be left alone.
4 OR HIGHER	10 OR HIGHER	16 OR HIGHER

TO KILL A
MOCKINGBIRD   TEXT
                                               QUEST

the world from behind the eyes of the character from your story. Once conversation wraps up, each group will then announce their decision to the class (drama!) and roll exactly one Role Playing Game dice to correspond with the decision their team has made.

Now for the fun part.

The EASY decision rolls a d8, the MEDIUM decision rolls a d12, and the HARD decision rolls a d20. But for each choice, there's a different success threshold that the dice roll must meet – so the easy dice roll might have to roll higher than, say, a 3 (giving a 5 out of 8 chance for success, or 62.5 percent odds of victory), while those groups that took the harder route might need to roll higher than, say, a 9 on the d12 (25 percent odds of success), or a 16 on the d20 (4 out of 20 = 20 percent chance of success). As with real life, with greater risk comes greater reward, which helps students feel the same emotion as the characters that they're getting to know about in your course content. Teachers can then award game points (or first pick of the day's activities) to the team with the highest roll, and student teams can keep track of their cumulative dice roll totals *multiplied by their total number of successful rolls* as you repeat the same daily warm-up procedure over the course of a longer unit to determine the overall "winner" of the game.

If you're looking to capture a splash of storytelling magic for any course or content area, this infinitely adaptable warm-up activity is a total game-changer. For the complete walkthrough (with fully illustrated slide templates!), check out EDrenalineRush.com/Resources.

Snake Oil

- **An #EDrenaline Rush Alternative To:** Humdrum character analysis

- **Feels Just Like:** Hawking your very own bootleg souvenirs

Off to Work We Go

Divide students into teams of no more than six. Have students write the names of random household objects on small slips of paper and pass them in for teacher collection. Shuffle the slips in a hat and then ask each group to select exactly TWO slips of paper.

Set the overhead timer for fifteen minutes and task groups with creating a "Snake Oil" product in which they mash-up the two common household items indicated on the slips of paper that they've selected. They should be imagined with the express intention of selling it to a particular historical or literary character from the current unit of study in your course content. Encourage students to be as "oily" with their sales pitches as they need to be, preying on specific character traits or weaknesses in an effort to sell this custom-made, junk product to this one and only buyer. (Example: How might a couch/broom combo product appeal to Abe Lincoln? Perhaps he'd need to "take a rest" after "sweeping up the remains of the Confederacy?")

If you'd like to check out a fantastic video tutorial on this classroom game, check out the YouTube page of my incredibly talented teacher friend Mrs. Stefanie Crawford (@MrsCford_tweets), tinyurl.com/CrawfordSnakeOil

A flyer from a student game called "Snake Oil,"
a combination refrigerator/toaster sold to
the two-timing protagonist of *Ethan Frome*

Questions for Discussion

1. What elements of a day in an amusement park are missing from this list of activities? How might you capture the feeling of those same experiences in your classroom?

2. Take a stroll through the toy aisle of your local Walmart or Target. What sorts of toys do you see on display? How might you leverage the same ideas that toy designers use in order to add life and excitement to your classroom?

3. Challenge yourself to complete a "blind date" activity design challenge. Pick up any old toy or game from that dusty shelf in the back of your closet and see how it feels to "fall in love" with this activity all over again. Could you turn a timeless classic like a Barrel of Monkeys into a classroom activity for your content area?

PART II:

Mud Runs

The family that I live for only breathes the air that smells of combat.

—The Ultimate Warrior, WWE Hall of Fame Wrestler

Chapter 4

Marathons, Mudders, and Spartans

It was somewhere around mile seven of the thirteen-plus mile 2016 Spartan Beast obstacle course race in South Carolina. The temperature was in the neighborhood of 82°F, and I was climbing a mountain, hauling a five-gallon bucket filled to the brim with about 100 pounds of rocks, when I said to myself, "These guys are genius. I paid *them* money to do yard work!"

Spartan Races are just one of a number of Obstacle Course Races ("OCR" for short, which also includes Tough Mudder, Warrior Dash, and Savage Race) that transform muddy off-road terrain races into giant obstacle courses and turn a mix of couch potatoes and weekend warriors into CrossFit enthusiasts and wannabe *American Ninja Warriors*. Part *Survivor* and part endurance race, some are more team-based or less aggressively competitive than others, but OCR events are one of the hottest participant tickets in sports today. In 2015, *USA Today* reported "annual participation [in OCR events has] surpassed that of traditional half and full marathons combined."

Shouldering forty-pound sandbags up and down double black diamond ski slopes.

Bear crawling face down in the mud through endless webs of barbed wire.

Diving into dumpsters filled with 6,000 gallons of freezing ice water.

These people were nuts. And I was loving every second of it.

Pride Goeth Before The Fall

I should probably back up for a bit here to clarify, because I'll never forget the way I initially reacted when I caught my first ever glimpse of a "just finished a marathon" athlete, shivering and huddling beneath a flimsy Mylar blanket. I was on a Metro train just after the Marine Corps Marathon in 2006, and I took one look at this sniveling, snot-covered, rain-and-sweat-drenched endurance runner and his dinky finisher's medal and thought, "All this for *that?* You have got to be kidding me."

Talk about a fixed mindset.

A few years later, I was playing in an indoor soccer rec league when I planted my leg in just the wrong way while charging for the penalty box. Total non-contact injury, but I hit the turf like I'd been shot by a bullet, immediately grabbing my right knee in pain. The nearest defender came over and asked if I was all right, to which I responded, "I think so. I just heard something pop." You should have seen the look on my face when he said, "I heard it pop, too, man—but I was standing *at midfield!*"

Many months and visits to the orthopedic surgeon later, my indoor soccer career was officially over. Even though I managed to avoid needing surgery, the doctors told me that I had no lateral movement left in my right knee, so any game that required quick pivots and side-to-side activity was simply out of the question.

Me in a wheelchair at Universal Studios, Florida,
in the summer of 2009.

This meant I could either sit around the house feeling sorry for myself, or I could find a new way to stay in shape. Team sports like soccer and basketball were out. But distance running? Well . . .

My transformation to Spartan Race and Tough Mudder loyalist was a long one. I started by signing up for a Turkey Trot 5K that took me a full fifty minutes to complete. That's a pace of sixteen minutes per mile, somehow even slower than the average time it takes to *walk* the exact same distance. I think I placed third to last overall, fifth if you count the two kids that a jogger dad was pushing in a stroller. It was humbling. It was hard. And it was the exact opposite of fun.

As I wheezed and snotted my way across the finish line, it hit me: In soccer, my win/loss ratio had just as much to do with how good I was as it did with how good my opponent had been. But in distance running? I wasn't racing against anybody else's time. I was racing against *myself.* So I was determined to do a better job the next time around. I signed up for another 5K. Then I spent sixteen weeks training for a ten-miler. And then, a full eighteen months after my inauspicious Turkey Trot debut, I ran my first marathon.

Ever play a game and come *so close* to success that it drives you to work that much harder the next time? You're not alone. In 1992, Thomas Gilovich, a psychology professor at Cornell, studied the body language, facial reactions, and post-competition interviews from medalists' Olympic Games – along with how these "near wins" affected these athletes subsequent performances. He found that even though the differences between first-, second-, and third-place finishers was literally down to the millisecond, silver medalists went on to be plagued by a feeling of "if only" thoughts about their near win, while bronze medalists—who may project satisfaction simply to be standing on the medal platform—often miss out on future medals altogether.

—The Rise: Creativity, the Gift of Failure, and
The Search for Mastery by Sarah Lewis

Now, getting back to that mountain in South Carolina . . .

Growth Mindset

At the crack of dawn or just before it on a dreary October morning in 2016, my brother Jeremy and my buddy Eric Russo piled into my trusty Ford Focus and began the 471-mile trek down from my home just outside of Washington, D.C., to the aptly named town of Spartanburg to compete in this thirteen-plus-mile mud race. The weather was brutal, and the six-hour drive (each way) was ridiculous. However, Spartan Race organizers offer athletes bragging rights and entry into an exclusive club called the "Spartan Trifecta" for anyone who manages to complete three different races of different lengths in a single calendar year. And since Eric, Jeremy, and I had already run two races of the shorter distance, we saw that elusive third piece of the pie as a genuine mark of accomplishment. It wasn't about the medal; it was about the growth!

In fact, distance running and obstacle course racing is and always has been a pure test of willpower and a battle of "you against *you*." Indeed, one might even say "it's the paradox that drives us all" (to borrow a few lines from the '80s power rock band Survivor's legendary anthem, "Burning Heart," made famous by the soundtrack of *Rocky IV*). And during so many of these crazy endurance runs, I'm often reminded of one of the most simple and profound motivational messages I first saw on the back of a fellow racer's t-shirt:

DLF > DNF > DNS.

In layman's terms?

A "dead last finish" is infinitely greater than "did not finish." And "did not finish" is greater than "did not start."

Achieving a Personal Record

Before the athletes take the course, Obstacle Course Races open with a bit of pomp and circumstance and a reminder that every new event is your chance to improve on your last performance. As the music blares and the smoke canisters ignite to shroud the starting lines of these events in a dense fog of blasting music, thick smoke, and pulsing adrenaline, there's always a hype man on site to help raise the stakes. My favorite pre-race ritual comes from the world of Tough Mudder, which asks everyone to take a knee and recite the Mudder pledge:

For a classroom teacher, there really couldn't
be a more perfect metaphor.

"The Tough Mudder is a challenge, not a race. I put teamwork and camaraderie before my course time. I do not whine; kids whine. I help my fellow Mudders complete the course. And I overcome all my fears."

The hype man continues, rattling off a laundry list of the type of obstacles that lay in store for competitors as soon as they cross the starting line with a promise: "We're gonna shock you, gas you, throw you into freezing water, and set you on fire!" But they are always mindful to add a word of comfort for first-time athletes or those who might be nervous about the course that awaits them: Even though you're taking part in the event to be your very best, you can always save a particular obstacle for another day on down the road. It's a powerful reminder to focus only on achieving your personal best. For, as *Chicago Tribune* columnist Mary Schmich once so eloquently observed, "The race is long, and in the end, it's only with yourself."

The adrenaline-fueled world of peak performance and OCR inspired me to create what I call a Personal Record scoring rubric. Just like a post-race obstacle debrief, the rubric offers an easy-to-read visual display of a student's sustained effort, improvement, and growth over time to provide a detailed look at which obstacles are causing each competitor the biggest problems. Pinpoint your weaknesses, and you can know where you'll need to train the hardest for your next big event.

Here's what it looks like:

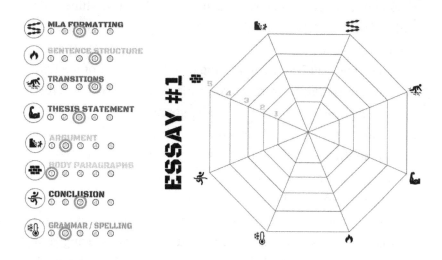

Take your traditional rubric and break it down into however many areas of focus you'll be scoring for that particular assignment. (In the case of the image above, I've pinpointed eight target areas for essay writing—but you can do as few or as many as you'd like.) For each target indicator, make a list from one to five and circle the corresponding score that the student has achieved for that particular "obstacle."

It's that simple.

When I hand back a scored assignment, I ask students to take a few moments to chart their performance on the spider graph immediately to the right of their scores. The end result creates a clear visual representation of each student's greatest areas of strength and weakness and provides an excellent starting point for self-reflection and their next round of training. To push students to the next stages of their growth, ask everyone to flip their Personal Record rubrics over and answer three questions to kick-start the next stages of their workout plan:

1. Which obstacle did you dominate? Why?
2. Which obstacle caused you the greatest challenge? Why?
3. What work do we still need to do to improve your performance on the toughest obstacle?

After students have had time to self-score and reflect, I'll collect the Personal Record rubrics and file them away until the next big "event" a few weeks down the line. And this time, I'll use a different colored pen for the scoring and pass the same score sheets back, so they can track their growth over time and repeat the self-reflection process.

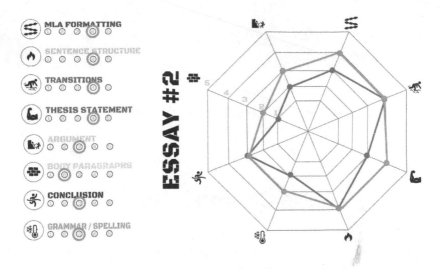

MLA FORMATTING
SENTENCE STRUCTURE
TRANSITIONS
THESIS STATEMENT
ARGUMENT
BODY PARAGRAPHS
CONCLUSION
GRAMMAR / SPELLING

ESSAY #2

Once students can see how they're growing and where they want to go next, the results are game-changing. Rather than being passive receptors of a teacher grade that might feel otherwise arbitrarily assigned, students are actively jumping right there alongside their instructor "in the trenches" of the obstacle course of our content. Suddenly, we're working together to hone our skills, digging through the details of where we fell short of our goals, and getting our hands dirty with personal plans for improvement.

If you'd like your own editable copy of the Personal Record rubric, visit EDrenalineRush.com/Resources.

The Champ is Here

For most Spartans and Tough Mudders, simply setting foot in the crazy world of obstacle course racing is enough of an adrenaline rush to last a lifetime. They're not there to collect achievement badges or win trophies—they're just trying to tackle whatever obstacles the course might throw their way, shave seconds off of their own personal best time, and prove to themselves that with enough hard work and perseverance, anything can be done. But when they cross the finish line? You'd better believe that quick vote of "congratulations" from a sideline volunteer and a finisher's medal can make a world of difference. Perhaps it's because, as my Canadian teacher friend Jason Howse once pointed out to me, "There's a reason that *Star Wars* didn't end with the Death Star blowing up. The award ceremony means something!"

To add an extra oomph to your finisher's medal rubrics of personal growth, consider adding a winner's trophy to celebrate those competitors who set course records.

High score on the latest unit exam? Take a selfie with a replica pro wrestling championship belt, and we'll post it on the class wall of honor! Crush a Breakout EDU or lay the Smackdown on

My mom (@dmeehan08), me, my brother-in-law Kenny, and my Dad at WrestleMania 35 at MetLife Stadium, just a few miles outside of New York City. Eighty-two-thousand cheering fans in attendance! Because even if you're a "big kid," sometimes it's a lot of fun to play pretend and be a part of the show.

a Socratic Seminar? Say cheese for a class photo hoisting the winner's trophy high for the whole world to see.

Or my personal favorite—create a series of collectible badges that students can win time and again for their particularly skillful displays of warrior spirit throughout the year.

Since I teach English, the badges I developed correspond with things like top-quality writing, MLA formatting, in-class presentations, or simply delivering a stand-out performance on a take-home assignment. If every day in my class was a new "race," then these were the "collectible trophies" beyond the simple finisher's medals, designed to recognize those individuals who really demonstrated high levels of grit, perseverance, or creativity with each new challenge.

I came up with ten different badges to collect in all, and so I picked up a bunch of printable stickers (those neon-colored Avery circular types available for $12 at Target) and printed out a single handout with the description of each of the awards and what it would take for students to earn them at any new challenge throughout the year. Knock our socks off with some inspired piece of peer revision? You just earned the Fur Trader badge! Made an excellent contribution to an online discussion? *Boom!* You're the proud owner of the Smooth Operator badge. You get the idea.

Naturally, we made a *big deal* of it each time a student earned a new badge, typically awarding no more than two to three badges for outstanding work per week, complete with a mini award ceremony where students would be showered with a round of applause from their peers. Just like a mud run or a marathon, everybody who competes receives a "finisher's medal," but for the "winner" of the race? Well, it's only fitting that they get something more to recognize their efforts.

Hokey? No doubt. But effective beyond my wildest dreams. Here's an actual parent email on the heels of one of these rinky-dink "award ceremonies":

Mr. Meehan,

I just wanted to thank you for lifting [my daughter] up today. She wasn't having the best day. She was struggling. She texted and pleaded to come home early. I told her to gut it out, and maybe we could do some retail therapy later this week.

You, being the fantastic teacher that you are, gave her an award today that probably made her grow an inch taller. Really! She texted our family chat letting us know that "the coolest" thing happened to her today and explained it to us. She felt so proud.

Thank you! That little girl works so hard. School does not come easily for her. She juggles dance, Best Buddies, tons of homework, and math confusion on the daily. She really needed that encouragement.

Thank you!

Keep doing what you're doing! Please teach seniors, too, so she can have you next year!

People compete in marathons, mud runs, and OCRs for all sorts of reasons, spending countless months in training and willingly taking on whatever challenges the course might throw their way, in spite of whatever private battles they may be fighting. This parent's email is just one example of the kind of daily struggles that our students face that would have gone *completely unnoticed* in a traditional classroom environment! Positive relationships are the

foundation of great teaching. Instead of sitting by idly as a scripted lesson plan unfolds around them, students get a powerful sense of belonging when they can see that their effort in the classroom can change the very nature of the day's instruction. And if something as simple as an "Attagirl!" award sticker is enough to make this student feel seen, appreciated, and empowered?

Sign. Me. Up.

Extreme Challenges

In the summer of 2014, the ALS foundation developed the ingenious "ice bucket challenge." Folks around the world took social media by storm, gleefully dumping buckets of ice over their heads and challenging others to do the same to join them in the fight against Lou Gehrig's disease. Since the money went to a great cause, most people who took the ice bucket challenge actually went ahead and donated in addition to posting their viral video. The ALS foundation wound up raising a staggering $115 million in a single year, exceeding even the most ambitious expectations of the project's success.

Mixing extreme obstacles with social shareability and at least a little bit of human vanity, OCR organizers position photographers in prime locations to document the most visually striking challenges. Two- and three-person teams hoist logs weighing several hundred pounds high on their shoulders. Acrobatic super athletes swing from spinning monkey bars while suspended over giant pools of mud! Competitors plunge straight into dumpsters, packed to the brim with ice water, or charge headlong into a field of dangling wires to deliver 10,000-volt electric shocks! These make for great pictures. And in an era of social media, a picture truly can speak a thousand words.

Get Cracking! In March of 2019, I led a teacher PD day where we filmed a 30 second snippet of a room full of grown-ups taking part in a demo game that would go on to become The #EggDashChallenge. I shared the video on Twitter and, in less than a month's time, the post had racked up 75,000 views and inspired high-energy videos of teachers organizing all sorts of #EggDashChallenge variations in classrooms of their own, with colorful game-changing "egg-tivities" in 40 US states, 6 Canadian provinces, and 10 countries around the world. You never know what sort of classroom activity video might go viral!

So grab a camera! And encourage your students to do the same. The "shock value" of sharing high-energy photos from events on school websites, class Twitter feeds, teacher YouTube channels, or student Snapchat stories can add life, adrenaline, and excitement to any classroom. The rest of this chapter plays like a giant obstacle course, offering up a "dirty dozen" kinesthetic activities that would feel right at home in a Spartan Race or an episode of *Survivor*!

#EggDashChallenge

- **Designer:** John Meehan (@MeehanEDU)

- **An #EDrenaline Rush Alternative To:** Traditional quiz or review activity

- **Feels Just Like:** Breakneck speed baseline sprints at basketball practice

Survivors Ready? Go!

Write out a bunch of numbered question items and cut them apart into small strips so there is exactly one question on each strip of paper. Place the numbered questions into plastic Easter eggs (one question per egg) or crumple up paper balls and store the stack of eggs at the front of your classroom.

Set a timer on the overhead board. Students are allowed to retrieve one plastic egg from the pile at the front of class at a time, taking it back to their desk and opening the egg to reveal the question it contains (no "texting and driving," so to speak). If a student doesn't know the answer to the question they have selected or feels that the question is too hard, they are welcome to take that numbered item back to the front of the classroom and drop it off in exchange for a new one, but they do so at the expense of

precious seconds lost in the effort to complete as many numbered questions as they can before time expires. Add an extra layer of scaffolding to your game by color-coding questions by difficulty, or "plus" it with an extra degree of intrigue by assigning hidden point values to different questions, which are only revealed once the time has expired.

To see the original viral video and read the full story behind this activity, visit EDrenalineRush.com/Resources.

Anchor Chart Keep-Away

- **Designer:** John Meehan (@MeehanEDU)

- **An #EDrenaline Rush Alternative To:** Sustained silent note-taking. Add instant teamwork and strategy to anchor charts!

- **Feels Just Like:** A giant game of keep-away

Survivors Ready? Go!

Divide students into four teams. Give each team a giant sheet of anchor chart paper and assign a content-related prompt. This is their chance to brain dump as much as they can about the assigned topic into a massive list of bullet point items. The team with the most items on their anchor chart when time expires wins.

But there's a catch: Everyone in class is openly encouraged to try to catch a peek at the work products of rival groups as they build their own anchor charts. Protect your team's intel and steal as much information from rival groups as you can!

Human shields, scouts, spies—you name it! One time, I even had a particularly savvy exchange student volunteer to write all of the notes for her team in Mandarin! All's fair in love and war. Super high-energy, collaborative, and competitive, this is a great way to liven up any unit where you've got a ton of information to review.

Floor is Lava

- **Designer:** John Meehan (@MeehanEDU)

- **An #EDrenaline Rush Alternative To:** Traditional worksheets or quizzes

- **Feels Just Like:** Everyone's favorite imagination game from childhood

Survivors Ready? Go!

Take a traditional quiz or worksheet and cut each question apart into an individual slip. Assign each question a specific point value and tuck the question inside an oversized manila envelope. Write a giant number anywhere from one to three on the outside of the envelope and scatter envelopes on the floor, so you'll have created what looks like a giant classroom game of Twister.

Set an overhead countdown timer. Students must find a way to stand on any envelope of their choice. The giant numbers on the outside of the envelope indicate the total number of people who can stand with them on that particular envelope. But the floor is lava! So students must huddle up closely and help hold one another up to make sure that no one is touching anything but the envelope beneath his or her feet.

At the end of the countdown, students work with anyone else who stood on their particular envelope to solve the problem it contains (and earn its hidden point values). Rinse and repeat over multiple rounds and feel free to mark penalty point deductions for anyone who falls into the lava. Make subsequent rounds that much harder by reducing the number of envelopes marked with "1."

Trench Warfare

- **Designer:** Courtney Lewicki (@LewickiEDU)

- **An #EDrenaline Rush Alternative To:** A traditional centers activity

- **Feels Just Like:** Building a fort out of couch cushions or snow

Survivors Ready? Go!

Divide students into two teams on opposite sides of the classroom. Set an overhead timer for exactly five minutes and inform the student teams that they will have exactly that amount of time to construct their army's barracks (using old newspaper and tape) for a full-class game of trench warfare.

Place a small rectangular bucket or cardboard box in the center of the classroom, midway between the two, newly constructed, army barracks of newspaper and student desks. This area between the two rows of student desks will serve as "no-man's-land" today, which all students must pass through in order to reach "the drop zone" by placing work products in the bucket.

Divide a traditional worksheet into four to six smaller stations, placing exactly half of the stations as "battle zones" available behind each barracks. As students crouch behind the sight lines of their newspaper fortresses, they'll have to work together with teammates to solve each of the prompt questions at the stations provided. Since only half of the questions will ever be on one side of the class at a time, students will have to find a way to get across the classroom by army crawling or waiting for a timely distraction when the teacher "isn't looking" (wink) to make their way across no-man's-land and collect the other half of the question set that's been scattered on the opposite end of the divide. Students will use the bucket in the middle of the classroom to drop off all assigned work products when they are completed, which guarantees that everyone will take part in the activity.

Remind student teams that they are all soldiers in the same army, working against the watchful eyes of the enemy detection (that's you) for the day, and that means that they will have to get comfortable in crowded spaces and avoid being spotted by the teacher as they make their way back and forth across the battlefield. Use your best teacher judgment to find strategic reasons to be "distracted" set off in parentheses or dashes to create opportunities for students to sneak back and forth across the classroom "without you noticing," and keep the game interesting by occasionally spotting a particularly daring soldier just as they are about to make their dramatic escape. You might even encourage students to help each other out in a good-natured bit of teamwork with the teacher distractions or consider adding a three-shot policy with sticker trackers (e.g., "grazed," "wounded," "dead") to keep the discouragement down and the energy high!

No-Man's-Land

- **Designer:** Kathleen McDermott

- **An #EDrenaline Rush Alternative To:** Any activity where students need to review

- **Feels Just Like:** Old school gym class dodgeball

Survivors Ready? Go!

Push desks into two clear rows, creating a massive aisle in the middle of the classroom. Students will complete this activity while standing behind these desk rows or being seated on the floor in the areas behind them. Remove all other desks from the field of play by pushing them to the back of the room or the edges of your classroom walls.

Divide students into two opposing teams and have them take their places behind the front lines of the row of desks that serve as the "front lines" of their team's camp. Place two buckets in the no-man's-land area between the two desk rows and cut up a series of numbered questions from an existing test, quiz, or review activity. The goal of the activity is to work with teammates to solve one question at a time and complete the entire question set before the opposing team does the same. All of the questions for each team to solve start out by being placed in your team's bucket in the no-man's-land area of the game, so students will constantly need to keep sending brave soldiers into the field of battle in order to retrieve questions for their respective teams in order to progress in the game.

Let students know that anyone in the no-man's-land area is open season to receive enemy fire and encourage students to use crumbled snowballs of paper as their ammunition to fire on enemy targets as they bravely make their way into the no-man's-land area. Soldiers are welcome to use their own notebooks to deflect incoming fire, but any student who receives three or more direct hits will have to head to the medical tent (the teacher's desk), where they will have to correctly answer a one-on-one question related to course content and posed by the teacher, before making their way back into the field of battle.

Paper Snowball Fights

- **Designer:** Unknown

- **An #EDrenaline Rush Alternative To:** Any traditional writing prompt and share-out activity

- **Feels Just Like:** The world's coolest study hall prank

Survivors Ready? Go!

Students write down individual questions for discussion or specific unit concepts on individual sheets of notebook paper before crumpling them up into balls. On the teacher's signal, the class transforms into an all-out snowball fight, with papers flying in all directions for precisely the duration of a teacher countdown. Once the countdown reaches zero, students grab the nearest paper snowballs and respond to the prompt questions. This same activity works great as a creative writing exercise when encouraging students to write down words at random related to a particular theme, which they can then turn into "quick writes" in the form of a haiku or other themed creative writing prompts.

Firestarter

- **Designer:** Kathleen McDermott and John Meehan (@MeehanEDU)

- **An #EDrenaline Rush Alternative To:** Traditional activities where students have to develop their own questions

- **Feels Just Like:** A high-stakes fire-building challenge on *Survivor*

Survivors Ready? Go!

Grab a bag of wooden blocks. Divide students into four teams and have them work together with their teammates to generate higher order thinking (H.O.T.) questions related to your specific unit of study or course content. Set an overhead timer for 10 minutes.

Each time a student team can successfully write a H.O.T. question, they should raise their hand to call over the teacher, who will review the question for a quick quality control check. If the question is written to standard, the team receives a wooden building block to help represent the growing materials they're using to "build the fire." But if the question is not completed to standard, the team will lose a building block to represent a failed attempt at sparking deeper conversation with a well-developed H.O.T. question. When time expires, the team with the tallest tower wins!

Badge Battles

- **Designer:** John Meehan (@MeehanEDU)

- **An #EDrenaline Rush Alternative To:** The usual peer review routine

- **Feels Just Like:** Collecting merit badges from your days in the Scouts

Survivors Ready? Go!

Divide your existing scoring rubric into a set number of stations with one station for each of the assignment's particular "look for" areas for improvement. Examples might include active versus passive voice, MLA formatting, or correctly using text evidence to support a claim. Assign a separate colored badge or symbolic icon for each station.

Set a timer for ten minutes and have students meet up with two or three classmates at the station of their choice. Working with their peers, students review one another's work products to rate and score the target skill assigned to that station. They should focus only on the specific indicator that corresponds with that particular station. Once time expires, students vote amongst themselves in each station to determine which work product was strongest, second strongest, and third strongest. Each student then collects a corresponding token from that station as a mark of their achievement.

Students then shuffle groups to new stations for review and work with different sets of partners to correct and reflect on one another's work products through the lens of the next available skill or concept-specific station for review. Repeat the countdown process and the student voting at the conclusion of the countdown, so students can have a clear visual idea of where exactly their draft is succeeding and where specifically it still might require the most work. (For example, an individual student might have a first-place badge for MLA formatting but only a third-place badge for quote integration. And just like that, the student knows to focus the bulk of their revisions on text evidence.)

King of the Hill

- **Designer:** Renee Henderson (@MsReneeScience)

- **An #EDrenaline Rush Alternative To:** Ho-hum teacher-led review activities

- **Feels Just Like:** The classic playground game—with less chance of injury!

Survivors Ready? Go!

Circle up the desks and place one seat in the center of the ring. Nominate one student to take a place in the center seat—they are now the "King (or Queen) of the Hill." Students in the surrounding perimeter now take turns, one at a time, peppering this student with questions regarding the current unit of study or related course content. "King of the Hill" scores a point for each question he or she is able to answer correctly (as determined by the teacher). If the King of the Hill gets stumped by a particular student's question, that student trades places with the student who posed the question that stumped them. The game continues with a new student in the center of the circle, scoring points as before. At the end of the time limit, the player with the most points scored is declared the winner.

Attack the Barracks

- **Designer:** John Meehan (@MeehanEDU)

- **An #EDrenaline Rush Alternative To:** Any assignment that requires lots of otherwise mundane instances of compliance-level work products that need quick rounds of teacher review (e.g., note card formatting, citations in a bibliography, massive tables of scientific data / square roots, etc.)

- **Feels Just Like:** Making a mess with LEGO towers and gleefully knocking them down

Survivors Ready? Go!

Divide students into four teams. The goal of the activity is for each team to build the most visually impressive LEGO structure possible, but they can only earn additional bricks by submitting sets of work products completed to standard. Set an overhead timer. Students can work together with their peers to assemble a collection of (x) number of properly formatted work products, which they can then bring to the teacher for review. (I like to set the "x" at exactly ten work products per submission; that way you are not constantly bombarded with one-off questions at once.)

Once a student team has collected their set of ten work products to standard, they send a representative to the teacher desk for a spot-checking work product review. If all ten of the student submissions are correctly formatted to standard, the student rolls a six-sided die at the teacher's desk and uses the scoop of that size to obtain additional LEGO bricks for the group to use in their construction efforts. (A dice roll of one equals the smallest scoop, and a dice roll of five is rewarded with the largest scoop. Students who roll a six get the added bonus of grabbing a full handful of LEGO bricks using their hand!) Then it's back to the group for more formatting and group work product discussion, and you can keep the ball rolling with a perpetual motion cycle of peer review.

For a more detailed look at this activity, visit EDrenalineRush.com/Resources.

Rally Coach Relay

- **Designer:** John Meehan (@MeehanEDU) and @KaganOnline

- **An #EDrenaline Rush Alternative To:** Traditional worksheets

- **Feels Just Like:** A relay race through course content

Survivors Ready? Go!

The Kagan approach to the "Rally Coach" activity pairs students in two-person teams. In a traditional Rally Coach activity, one student writes the answers to the question while their partner serves as the "coach," offering tips and problem-solving suggestions as they go. Typically, students will trade roles once (x) number of questions are complete (all of the questions in a single row of addition problems, for example).

Add instant adrenaline to this approach by making the paired activity a team-vs-team relay race, where partners must work together by trading off roles, back and forth, as they make their way through a full worksheet or multi-page Google Form. And while the first team to complete the form "wins" access to a "bonus level" (read: enrichment questions), each team is motivated to support their teammates and complete their assignment in class before time expires. Teachers get to serve as "referees" to make sure that teammates are helping one another and playing by the rules accordingly—reserving the right to offer on-the-fly clarification questions to groups who are particularly fast-moving to make sure the game stays competitive throughout.

Clothespin Bumper Cars

- **Designer:** Kat Bynum (@KBynumEDU)

- **An #EDrenaline Rush Alternative To:** Traditional review activity where the teacher would have to call on students one at a time

- **Feels Just Like:** Battle Mode from *Mario Kart* without the turtle shells!

Survivors Ready? Go!

Set a five-minute timer and break students into teams of 4-5. Each student will have exactly five minutes to work with their teammates and write as many closed-ended review questions on your current unit of study as they possibly can. (Students can use lined paper or submit their questions to a single question Google Form, but each student should have his or her own list to carry with them for this activity.) Students don't need to write out the answers to these questions—but they *do* need to know the answer to any question they write down—since they'll only be allowed to ask questions they've included on their list when they enter the Bumper Car area. Giving students time to work together writing questions in teams helps everyone coach each other up and better prepare for the student-centered content review "Battle." And using the team-vs-team approach helps students hold one another accountable since nobody wants to be the weakest link! While teams are writing down their questions, distribute three clothespins (or paper-clips, etc.) to each student in the class.

Clear all of the desks to the side of the classroom, so you'll have created a giant "pool." Reset your timer for five additional minutes, and have each student clip their three clothespins onto their sleeves to begin the game. For five fast-paced minutes, students may move about the classroom freely while asking content-related questions of their fellow classmates. Get a question wrong, and you must surrender one of your clothespins to a rival. Lose all three clothespins and you're out of the game. Last player standing wins—or the student with the most clothespins remaining when time expires is declared the winner.

Questions for Discussion

1. Obstacle course racers take pride in conquering extreme challenges in pursuit of personal records. How might you be able to make use of a personal record rubric, like the spiderweb chart discussed in this chapter, in your classroom to get students thinking beyond traditional grades?

2. Think of a core set of 6-10 routine skills that your class revisits time and again throughout the school year (timed writings, translation exercises, speaking activities, etc.). Is there a way you might be able to develop some sort of "badge" system to recognize students for their continued growth in these core skills?

3. Are there activities in your classroom that might easily lend themselves to "extreme photos" like OCR obstacles or the Ice Bucket Challenge? How might you share these images with parents and families to drive even further levels of student engagement?

Chapter 5

The Ultimate Obstacle

*Perhaps the greatest skill in a teacher
is their ability to distinguish between
"I taught it" and "they learned it."*

—John Wooden

Sometimes, the biggest obstacles are the ones we build up in our own minds. One of the hallmarks of most mud races is their love of constructing sprawling spiderweb-like mazes of barbed wires or building elaborate fields of electricity where competitors must brave their way beneath dangling coils of 10,000-volt electric shocks. Daring competitors love to army crawl their way through these tangled networks of twisted metal; these bad boys are not for the faint of heart. And due to the sheer promise of pain that these visually assaulting challenges present, even the boldest competitors can't help but think that certain obstacles might just be a little *too* extreme. There's a reason why race organizers have you sign a waiver before the event, right?

Let's be clear: There is no world in which a responsible teacher should try their hands at creating school-friendly mazes using military-grade barbed wire. But that doesn't mean our classrooms are without their very own extreme obstacles in the eyes of the students we serve.

Ever heard of the Socratic Seminar?

It's the very definition of the student-centered classroom, yet it remains one of the most fear-inspiring obstacles in all of education. After all, what well-meaning administrator hasn't encouraged their faculty to "try a Socratic Seminar"? What teacher among us hasn't gone white with fear at the prospect of giving our students the proverbial keys to the car before we're even sure that they can drive it? And what student in the world hasn't felt an all-too-familiar and deep-seated flash of panic like that described in this satirical article from *The Onion*, with the headline, "Oh God, Teacher Arranged Desks in a Giant Circle"?

> *OVERLAND PARK, KS—Appearing stunned and unsettled as they entered her classroom Wednesday, students from Ms. Frederickson's fourth-period social studies class were reportedly overcome with panic upon discovering that, oh God, all the desks had been arranged in a giant circle. 'I have no idea what's going to happen here, but it can't be good,' said a visibly shaken Katie Wahl, 11, who according to reports began steeling herself for whatever god-awful group project, class discussion, or sharing of personal experiences the sixth-grade teacher might have in store for them.*

If everyday classroom activities were fun runs, then the Socratic Seminar is the BEAST—the biggest, baddest, and most daunting challenge around. For many, a fully student-centered classroom presents the ultimate obstacle, striking fear into even the bravest who might stand in its presence, serving as a daunting reminder of just how quickly a classroom discussion can faceplant into a free-for-all shouting match.

But the Socratic Seminar doesn't have to be painful. If you're looking to make this student-centered pedagogy a regular part of your classroom instruction, there are a ton of resources and strategies available to help both teachers and their students feel safe and supported as they brave this uncharted maze of crossed wires and pointed exchanges.

Let's start with an easy training run to help get you warmed up.

Microlabs

- **Designer:** The National School Reform Faculty (@TheNSRF)

- **An #EDrenaline Rush Alternative To:** Otherwise directionless "turn and talk" or "think, pair, share" activities

- **Feels Just Like:** A low-impact practice conversation with three desks in a cluster

Survivors Ready? Go!

Set an overhead timer for between five and eight minutes. Break students into groups of three, with one or two student groups containing four members if absolutely necessary. Provide the entire class with a single prompt question that lends itself to multiple answers that can be supported with text evidence. Start the clock, and all students in all groups will then take a specific amount of time (sixty seconds works great for starters) to collect their thoughts and review their notes in preparation to answer the question.

When time expires, one student in each group ("Student A") takes the full amount of the next sixty seconds to offer their thoughts on the common prompt question that has been provided. Encourage students to use the entire time to make their arguments and resist the urge to race through the awkward silences. This method will encourage students to keep pushing their thinking with additional details in an effort to fully fill the allotted sixty seconds. When the time expires, reset the clock and have a second student in each group ("Student B") pick up the conversation. Doing this reserves their right to piggyback off of what has already been said, pivot their feedback in a different direction, or push back on some of the points that may already have been provided, again with all other group members frozen in silence for the duration of the student's allotted speaking time. After sixty seconds have expired, repeat the process a third time with "Student C."

Once all students have received the same amount of time to offer their positions or feedback on the current prompt question, use the remaining two to five minutes to encourage open table talk between group members. They'll now have the chance to dialogue freely with their group mates on the positions that each has already shared. (You can also use this time to allow those students who may be in oddball groups of four to likewise take a full minute of their own to offer their thoughts before the group breaks into a free exchange of ideas.)

It's a great way to warm up and develop the muscle memory and communication skills that will be required for the Ultimate Obstacle that is yet to come. Likewise, it helps students build confidence and the ability to work together with their peers in an effort to attack a common problem with multiple "barbs" that might have otherwise caught them by surprise. With some practice, your students will even develop the courage to jump right in to the proverbial twisted metal maze of a full-blown Socratic Seminar!

Game-Changing Dialogue

In the summer of 2015, I spent a few days at the University of Kansas and got a front row seat learning from the icon of instructional coaching, Dr. Jim Knight. One of the biggest themes of the week was the critical importance of building trust and empathy among instructional coaches and the teachers that we serve. And someone eventually boiled it down to a maxim that I repeat almost daily: "An instructional coach needs to *propose* not *impose*. Because that which you *impose* will be *opposed*."

> **"An instructional coach needs to *propose*, not *impose*. Because that which you *impose* will be *opposed*."**

It's essential for teachers and coaches to listen with genuine intent to understand, not to condone or to agree, but simply to let each individual know that their voice matters and their understanding of a situation—even if it is diametrically opposed to your own—is just as valid and has every bit as much right to be shared. That same sentiment is precisely why so many Socratic Seminars fall flat. Much like a barbed wire maze in an OCR, the only way to get people brave enough to jump into the fray is to reassure them that in spite of how menacing the activity might seem, they are absolutely safe and protected in the hands of well-trained officials to spot them at every step along the way. It wasn't too far of a logic jump to see that many of these very same principles could easily be applied to our work in classrooms with students, as well.

On Dr. Knight's recommendation as the conference adjourned, I picked up a copy of David Bohm's *On Dialogue* to read on the plane ride home. As I saw it, at the worst I was in for a slim, quick book that, if nothing else, gave me an excuse to fall asleep on a flight from Kansas City to D.C. Failing that, at least I could brag to my students that I'd spent my summer reading something by an honest-to-goodness quantum physicist.

But on the very first page, Bohm flipped the script on how I would forever approach class discussion.

Dialogue Versus Discussion

According to Bohm, too often we confuse "dialogue" and "discussion," and there's a critical difference between the two. Unlike a discussion, which shares the same root word as "concussion" (to shake together) and "percussion" (to strike forcibly), where the goal is literally to break something apart, an authentic "dialogue" is simply the free exchange of ideas, with no agenda other than to deepen one's own understanding through words. In fact, that's what the word "dialogue" literally means. It comes to us from the Greek *logos*, meaning "words," and *dia*, meaning not "two" but *through*.

Discussions are about winners and losers, hearing arguments for and against, breaking things down into small bits before ultimately pronouncing almighty judgment of right and wrong. But in a dialogue, there are no teams. We're playing together, so everybody wins if anybody wins.

Well dang. It's little wonder why nobody feels comfortable jumping into the Socratic Seminar! Going solo into a seminar is like staring down the razor-sharp web of a barbed wire maze: If it's a war of each against all, you feel totally stranded amid a sea of crisscrossing strands that can cut you to shreds. It's a terrifying prospect. For years I'd been treating my seminars like a discussion, when the activity was really supposed to be a team sport dialogue.

This sent my educator brain reeling: How much of traditional education is spent in discussion, where teachers hammer through rote talking points, systematically breaking down a text, smashing symbols, characters, and themes until our bleary-eyed students come around to what we believe are obvious and self-evident conclusions that neatly align with our own?

"Boo Radley is a mockingbird because ..."

"Gatsby's green light represents ..."

"Hamlet's tragic flaw is ..."

Clear your desks. Write in complete sentences. Eyes on your own paper. Ten points for each right answer. No, you may not use Google.

So it goes.

But how much time do we devote to cultivating authentic dialogue, as in give-and-takes like a team sport, with no right or wrong answers, where the teacher is just as surprised by the conversation as the students are and the only goal is to deepen a shared understanding of the subject? Or to use some snazzy educational jargon: How much time do we devote to classes where teachers are no longer "the sage on the stage, but a guide on the side"? What if educators started asking our students questions to which we didn't necessarily even have a clear answer in mind?

"How do you think Huck Finn would react to Black Lives Matter?"

"If Disney's Epcot built a Scotland-inspired *Macbeth* pavilion, what would it look like?"

"What apps might Willy Loman have on his iPhone?"

Use your notes? You bet. Text a friend? Why not? Suddenly, we're discovering together. It's safe to make mistakes. There's genuine curiosity. There's real learning. And there's joy. As teachers, we're used to being the founts of knowledge. But we have to learn how to be comfortable asking questions that are not easily answered—things that are easily answered are easily forgotten.

Maybe my Socratic Seminars were simply so-so because I was inadvertently pitting my students against each other. Maybe we failed because I kept expecting the same answers, or maybe I was just asking the wrong questions.

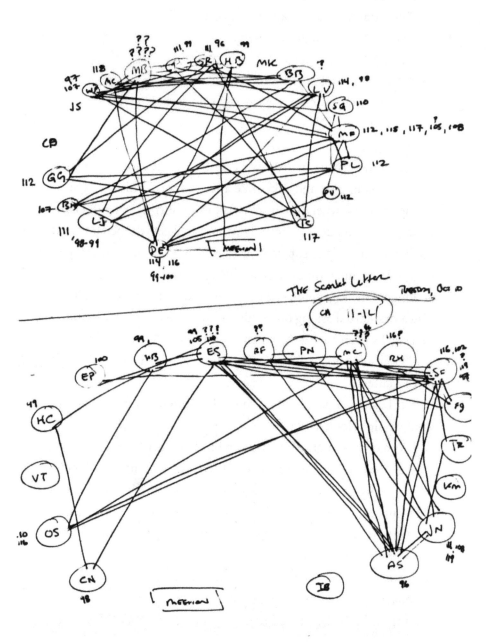

The Amazing Spider Web

For all the potential that these unbridled Socratic Seminars now seemed to present, I still struggled to figure out how to grade these sorts of activities. That's when my principal turned me on to *The Best Class You've Never Taught: How Spider Web Discussion Can Turn Students into Learning Leaders* by Alexis Wiggins (@AlexisWiggins), an educator, researcher, and daughter of the esteemed Grant Wiggins. In her fantastic book about all things Socratic Seminar, she offered the following advice: As students are taking part in a seminar, simply make a little map to chart the pattern of who's talking, connecting the dots as new students chime in to the dialogue, which will create something resembling a spider's web of the day's conversation. And when the seminar has concluded, take the spiderweb from that day's activity and present it to the class for further reflection.

Pretty cool, right?

Instead of telling students how well or how poorly *I* thought they'd done, the idea was simply to let students reflect on their performance as a class, based on the patterns in the spiderweb that *they* saw. Keeping track of multiple spiderwebs over time allows students to see signs of their progress and growth while keeping tabs on any new patterns that may emerge from the data. After all, this activity is meant to be a team sport.

I started making this change to my classroom in the fall of 2017. The results were instant and well-received, so by the time Thanksgiving rolled around, I figured I'd take advantage of Twitter's newly expanded character set to send a handful of shout-outs expressing my gratitude to all of the teachers and edtech products that had helped me level up my teaching game. A few hours later, I'd received a notification from a guy named Dave Nelson—who tweets under the username of @EquityMaps—and it read: "Maybe

#equitymaps has a chance to make your Things to be thankful for list next year? :)"

Oh great. Another edtech snake oil salesman, I thought. Who was this guy anyway? I scrolled back through my timeline. Turns out he had messaged me twenty-four hours prior: "Hi John . . . have you tried Equity Maps iPad app? Let the students map the web, show them, and see what happens."

Riding high on a mix of tryptophan from our Thanksgiving dinner and the leftover endorphins from a bunch of Twitter "likes" from my PLC teacher heroes, I bit the bullet and plunked down the $2.99 for whatever this "Equity Maps" nonsense was supposed to be. (Again, I feel the need to defend my skepticism here—as teachers are notoriously short on both time *and* money, there are a ton of conmen out there in the education space looking to make a quick buck off of an easy mark.)

Boy, was I wrong.

Equity Maps

Equity Maps is an app for the iPad designed to help facilitators keep track of who was talking in class and when. It's like a Fitbit for class participation. The interface was slick, and I was intrigued.

The app is pretty straightforward. Teachers start by using any one of the blank seating arrangement templates to assign individual user icons (male or female) for each student. It saves rosters, so you'll only ever have to do a bulk upload once per year. Once you're done adding session participants, you can click and drag the icons anywhere in the seating arrangement to show where each student is seated and start your class' Socratic Seminar.

Push the session record button, and the app will start keeping track of the class dialogue patterns using a built-in stopwatch timer. As each new student speaks, you simply tap the corresponding

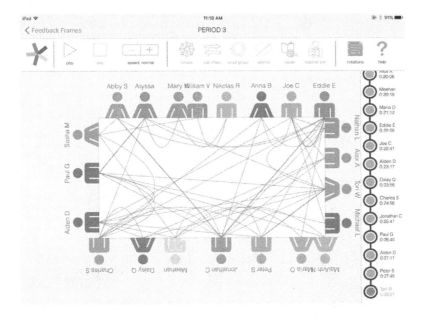

student's icon, and the app will automatically connect a line between each student and the one who spoke just before them— exactly as if you were drawing a spiderweb in a printed notebook. If you have an Apple TV or a connection dongle, you can project the session to your overhead in real time, so students can watch the spiderweb take shape before their very eyes.

Look Who's Talking

While the computer-drawn spiderweb map is neat to look at, it's in the aftermath of each session where Equity Maps becomes a can't-miss addition to any classroom. In addition to providing the visual map of how balanced the conversation may have been during that particular session, the app also gives you the ability to hit the play button, so you can watch a quick video playback to see the conversation web pattern unfolded in real time. With little effort, students can get a clear sense of who's talking, for how long, and when.

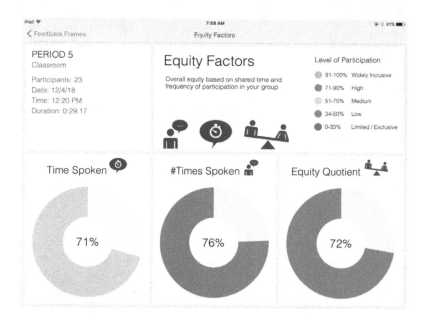

The app also features a series of point-and-click, look-for items, so teachers can easily push just one button to generate individual student reports with detailed items like who's citing specific examples from a text, asking great questions, or most effectively piggybacking off of earlier comments to drive the dialogue to deeper analysis and higher order thinking questions.

But my absolute favorite feature of the Equity Maps comes in the form of a feature it calls feedback frames. Feedback frames are automatically generated at the conclusion of each session, and offer a clear visual representation of how successful the overall seminar was in relation to the equity voice distribution as it was shared and fostered throughout the conversation.

I followed up with Dave Nelson, and he explained:

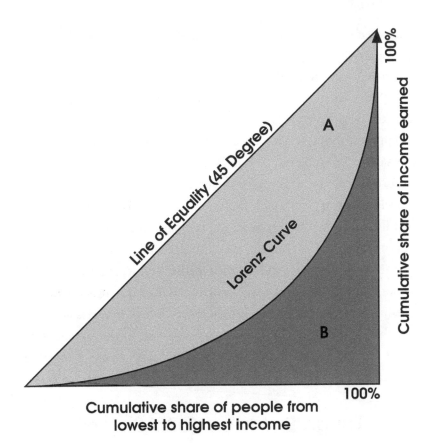

"The Equity Quotient is a way of looking at equity based on both time spoken and times spoken; we calculate the Gini coefficient of times spoken and time spoken and calculate the average based on 67 percent from Time Spoken, and 33 percent from Times Spoken. We've tried to create a way of looking at a combination of both with more emphasis on shared time."

The Gini Coefficient is a concept borrowed from the world of economics. In an equitable economy, 100 percent of people have access to 100 percent of the wealth. In a less equitable country, the number of people with access to that same amount of wealth can be much lower. The Gini Coefficient measures the distance between what is called the line of equality (the equal sharing of all resources between all members) and the Lorenz Curve (the actual distribution of wealth).

Since the data is so clear, succinct, and visually appealing, it makes for a fantastic start for the following spiderweb discussion to present the class with the screenshot findings from their previous effort, so students can reflect on where they succeeded and fell short in order to set goals for themselves and work towards higher levels of performance with each new seminar. And just like I'd felt while army crawling through the trenches in the Tough Mudder barbed wire mazes, I felt an incredible relief from recognizing the patterns of how these webs came together and what it took to conquer them. By studying their feedback frames, my students started feeling safe, supported, and encouraged to take new risks outside of their comfort zones. The obstacle was no longer as daunting as it had once appeared. My classes were finally working together as teams.

Tough Brudders (and Sisters!)

At the conclusion of each session, Equity Maps also provides a breakdown of how the conversation played out along gender lines, so classes can see data related to the percentage of time spoken by the average male student compared to the average amount of time spoken by a female student. This data led to some pretty eye-opening conversations, with one class being as far apart in the average time as far apart as forty-one seconds between male students and their female peers, which naturally led to some pretty heated discussions as we unpacked these findings together. One of my favorite moments came when Sam, a male student in my third period class, raised his hand to discuss this statistical anomaly:

"But Mr. Meehan. There are more guys than girls in this class! That's why those numbers are so far off from one another. Guys will always spend more time talking because there are just more guys in the room."

He was right—kind of. But very quickly, Mac, one of my super-savvy female students, raised her hand. With a smirk that would make Hermione Granger proud, Mac pointed out that while the *cumulative* total time spent talking by men might always exceed the time spoken by women, the *average* time spoken by any one member of the class should never be determined by that person's gender.

Even Sam had to chuckle at that one. Point taken.

When my eleventh grade American Literature classes made their way into a unit on early feminist authors of the late nineteenth and early twentieth centuries, the app was an invaluable resource regarding how much has changed about women and their role in society in the past 200 years. And before starting out on

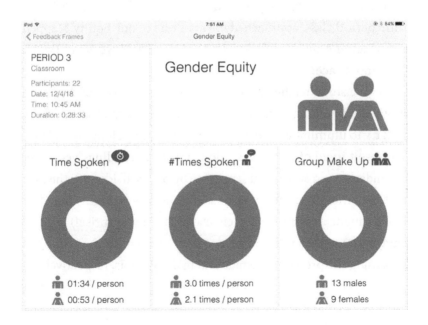

a day's conversation about the assigned readings, we took a cue from the world of OCRs by setting a collective, class-wide, Equity Map goal for ourselves of trying to get the difference between the average time spoken by a male student and a female student down to as close to zero seconds as we possibly could.

Check Your Privilege

The slogan of the Spartan Race cryptically invites first-timers to brave the world of these extreme competitions with the awe-inspiring promise that "You'll know at the finish line." Tough Mudder hype men start each race by asking participants a similar hypothetical question: "When was the last time that you did something for the first time?" Both of these muddy challenge events regularly dare participants to step outside of themselves to confront massive obstacles, to "do something every day that scares you just a little bit" in the effort to become a better, stronger version of yourself. I think that's why I was so impressed when we moved into our unit on the Harlem Renaissance, and Michael, a white student in my third period class, approached me after one of our Equity Mapped conversations and said, "Hey Mr. Meehan. Could we do an Equity Map about race?"

I gave students the option to vote on whether or not they were interested in taking part in an equity mapped conversation where we'd try to illuminate conversational discrepancy along racial lines. The result in all of my class sections was a resounding "yes" from all students, and so I let students, one by one, self-identify the race that they most commonly associated themselves with. (This data alone caught a number of their classmates by surprise!) And as students expressed their racial identity, I then coded them into the app, using the pre-coded female and male symbols, respectively, in order to create a binary division between students who identified as white and those who identified as persons of color.

For forty minutes, we concluded our unit on the Harlem Renaissance by discussing excerpts of poetry by Langston Hughes, Claude McKay, and Paul Laurence Dunbar. We waxed philosophically about nonfiction pieces by W.E.B. DuBois and Frederick Douglass, along with the narrative fiction of Ralph Ellison and the opening chapter of *Invisible Man*. And we touched on contemporary sociological studies and research that ranged from the Harvard Implicit Bias Test to Black Lives Matter and Peggy McIntosh's groundbreaking essay, "The Invisible Knapsack: Unpacking White Privilege."

I've never seen teenagers so genuinely invested in listening and having dialogue with their peers. We didn't score a perfect division between white and non-white students (though we were close with an average of about four seconds between the two groups), but it was one of the single most enriched and productive conversations our class had ever experienced. White students openly acknowledged the cultural benefits they are afforded, simply by virtue of their skin color. Students of color empathized with one another and explained the challenges of being born a minority in a culture that so often marginalizes them. White students likewise posed genuinely thoughtful questions of their non-white peers, asking what they might be able to do in order to acknowledge their privilege and extend it to others who may not have been born with these same invisible benefits. And students of mixed ancestry contributed enthusiastically, discussing how easy it is for some of them to don the knapsack of white privilege while at other times expressing heartfelt solidarity with their darker-skinned classmates whose complexion did not afford them the same luxury.

Socratic Seminars can be scary enough obstacles, but getting a room full of students to open up in front of their peers and explore deeper issues of race, privilege, and unconscious biases? That takes next-level guts from all parties involved, and there is no way I could have done it alone.

Equity Maps is a game changer.

Questions for Discussion

1. Have you used a Socratic Seminar or a variation of it in your classroom? If it's working for you, what makes it work? If you haven't used it, what has stood in the way of its success in your classroom?

2. How might your classes' Socratic Seminar efforts improve if the pattern, depth, and nature of their last conversation's engagement was presented in a visual dashboard just before a new one was about to begin?

3. In your professional practice, ask yourself, "When was the last time you did something for the first time?" What is one academic obstacle that you've always wanted to conquer? What's holding you back?

Chapter 6

Building Your Tribe

Every morning in Africa, a gazelle wakes up. It knows it must outrun the fastest lion, or it will be killed. Every morning in Africa, a lion wakes up. It knows it must run faster than the slowest gazelle, or it will starve. It doesn't matter whether you're the lion or a gazelle—when the sun comes up, you'd better be running.

—Christopher McDougall, *Born to Run*

My longtime teacher friend Eric (@erusso78) is pretty awesome. Just ask him, and he'll be more than happy to tell you. Born and raised in a large Italian family in New Jersey like mine, he is fast-talking, hard-working, and ridiculously good at what he does for a living. He's also one heck of a cook, a pretty mediocre fantasy football player, and a long-suffering fan of the New York Jets—but those are stories for another book.

The team of "Teach, Run, Repeat" at the finish line of the
Great Allegheny Passage Relay in October of 2018. From
left to right, me, Derek Long, Ed.D. (@DerekLong929), Brice
Hostutler, NBCT (@brice78), and Eric (@erusso78)—three
of the strongest teachers I've ever met.

I first met Eric in the summer of 2010, when we were selected
to join a fifty-two-member cohort of wide-eyed career switchers
and energetic young guns in a six week crash course of educator
training through The New Teacher Project (TNTP). After just a
little over thirty days of "teacher bootcamp," we started working
in public schools scattered throughout Prince George's County,
Maryland, one of the country's lowest performing school districts.
Looking back, I don't really remember exactly the first thing Eric
said to me, but I'm 99 percent sure that it was an insult about my
taste in brown bagged lunches.

We've been close friends ever since.

Together, Eric and I have run something like a dozen or so races. Starting with the Cherry Blossom 10 Miler in Washington, D.C., and working our way through a respectable slate of half marathons, Tough Mudders, and Spartan Races in nearly a half dozen different states. Sometimes we'll conscript his wife, Nicole, my cousin, Mariana (a personal trainer and a Boston Marathon qualifier), or my brother, Jeremy, to join in the fun. One time Eric even convinced me to join him and two other teacher friends for the Great Allegheny Passage relay, a two-day, four-person, round-the-clock trail run where each member of the team logs something crazy like thirty-plus miles of running in a 150-mile race from the Cumberland Gap of Maryland to the steely streets of Pittsburgh, Pennsylvania.

While the race distances and the course obstacles are extreme, there's something to be said about the appeal of these crazy events that has a lot to do with the power of developing what almost feels like a "tribe" of warriors to join you in battle. In fact, many of the obstacles are literally impossible to conquer by one's lonesome, and so it's not an uncommon sight to see somebody asking a teammate to lend a hand in a road race, offer a cheer from the sidelines, or ask for the chance to stand on top of a friend's shoulders (or head) as they try to make their way over a muddy embankment.

Rise and Grind

Marathons and OCRs are punishingly long distances that put brutal amounts of stress on participants' minds and bodies while demanding every available ounce of their mental toughness. To perform at one's personal best, these events require months of preparation, proper diet, careful training, and a tremendous degree of dedication. And if you cheat your workouts along the way, it's all but guaranteed that you'll suffer the consequences on race day and in the weeks that follow.

I look at teaching the same way: It's a full-tilt commitment to bringing my absolute best to my classroom for the full slate of 180 instructional days. And I won't lie to you. Like many a 5 a.m. workout, there are some weeks where cobbling together a Friday class newsletter, finessing the finer points of a themed rubric, or putting the finishing touches on a high energy lesson plan is the absolute *last* thing I want to do. It takes time. It takes intentionality. It takes discipline. And it takes a tremendous degree of sustained effort.

Let's face it: There is an incredible amount of work expected of classroom teachers of all ages and grade levels. But would you rather put the work in before "race day" or recover from it? You either put the work in on the front end, or you feel it on the back end.

> **Let's face it: There is an incredible amount of work expected of classroom teachers of all ages and grade levels. But would you rather put the work in before "race day" or recover from it? You either put the work in on the front end, or you feel it on the back end.**

School is a team sport. And your tribe is counting on you.

The effort that I put in to high-energy lesson planning is time that I don't have to spend dealing with bored students, angry parents, and disappointed administrators. Is it exhausting? Without question. But every second I spend fine-tuning a high-energy lesson plan is another minute I don't have to spend fighting against the forces of inertia and students cutting class, forgetting their homework assignments, or half-heartedly copying their answers from a classmate. For every YouTube video that I'm posting *live as it unfolds* while students are kicking butt in the classroom, I'm helping parents and family members see that their children are safe and supported. I'm celebrating these young scholars by providing play-by-play footage of them dominating the course content right there in the trenches as if they were professional athletes! And for every over-the-top educational obstacle course I'm cooking up for my curriculum, I'm helping my students get fired up to achieve the impossible.

The way I see it, my students, their families, and my administrators are my teammates—and by completing the work we assign, entrusting us with the care of their children, and providing as many physical or digital resources that they can afford, they have absolutely held up their leg of the race. For better or worse, families send us the best that they've got, period. They're not keeping better students at home! Knowing that I have to keep designing, improving, and properly maintaining a high-energy classroom environment so that things stay in good working order each week absolutely holds me accountable to do the same. That means sharing the good news about how these kids are crushing it

in the classroom, offering regular opportunities for my students to provide reflections and feedback on how our class is meeting their myriad learning needs, and steering clear of killing any of their momentum with lame-o lesson plans that might otherwise have gotten stuck in the mud of a "Death by PowerPoint" trap.

Just like a race official, it's our job to make sure that the participants in our courses are safe, supported, cheered for, encouraged, and never too far from a proverbial water break or a word of encouragement when they need one. That's why I flood my Twitter feed and YouTube page with daily updates of the incredible stuff that my students are doing. I fire off a fully illustrated course newsletter every Friday to let families know how their students are crushing it in the classroom. I'm crazy proud of all the work that they're putting in, so I use social media whenever possible to celebrate their triumphs and make them feel like the academic super athletes they are. Sharing a weekly highlight reel with students and their families is like a twenty-first-century take on posting a gold star paper on the refrigerator!

If you'd like to adapt any of these resources for your own class, head on over to EDrenalineRush.com/Resources.

We're all a part of the same tribe.

Ready, ECET, Go!

A few years back, Eric was working as a member of the Teacher Advisory Council for the Bill and Melinda Gates Foundation. He had a big hand in helping to organize the Foundation's "Elevating and Celebrating Effective Teachers and Teaching" (ECET2) national conference in New Orleans, Louisiana, so I gladly accepted his invitation to join these folks for a few days in the Big Easy to talk shop and improve our craft. Like runners, teachers are stronger together. Eric made a point of giving me a head's up before the conference started. "John," he said, "we've got a bunch of great sessions lined up. But I think you'll really want to meet Chris Bronke." Christopher Bronke (@mrbronke) is a high school English teacher at Downers Grove North High School in Downers Grove, Illinois. These days, when he's not busy in his classroom, he serves as the Director of the National Blogging Collaborative (NBC). He founded the group with a handful of like-minded educators at the National ECET2 conference in 2014, which has gone on to become a network of coaches to support fellow educators in the writing process. As the NBC website explains, "NBC cultivates and supports the capacity of all educators to use their unique voice to elevate the craft of teaching and learning."

At ECET2 NOLA, Chris was coming off of a rather impressive write-up from *The Atlantic* in which his classroom application of Twitter was receiving glowing reviews. The idea felt ripped right out of the playbook of a choose-your-own adventure obstacle course, and it is just too good not to share:

Turn your nightly reading assignments into a hashtagged conversation.

Whoa.

My students went wild over this homework format, to the point where it's become a yearly staple of our novel study for at least two or three units each year. It's a snap to set up, too: Just have students create Twitter accounts specifically for school, pick a handful of hashtags at the start of a new unit, and let your students go to town with their nightly annotations. Instead of reading solo, students use Twitter to share written thoughts, photos of their annotated pages, memes inspired by the content they're reading, and links to relevant videos or websites that can help fellow students make sense of the assigned material. Suddenly, nightly homework discussions start to feel like a social hour with your tribe—and you're simultaneously teaching your assigned course content while modeling twenty-first-century literacy skills.

Sometimes, it helps to offer a bit of heads-up before stepping into an uncharted arena to let your tribe know that even though the event might push you to extremes, at no time will you ever have to feel like your health or safety is at risk. For this reason, Tough Mudder makes a point of publishing a map of course obstacles (and the water stations) in the days before an event to help runners plan their strategies on how best to conquer the course. Likewise, pre-selecting a series of themed hashtags before you start a unit makes slicing and dicing the data a breeze for your class discussions and jigsaw activities. At the start of our three week unit on *Adventures of Huckleberry Finn*, for example, my students make note of the six hashtags outlined below:

- #HuckLies—Moments where Huck (or any other character) is "stretching" the truth
- #HuckFree—Tweets relating to freedom (or lack thereof)
- #HuckRace—Text examples dealing with racism or racist attitudes
- #HuckLearns—Twain satirizing a character's ignorance or the education system
- #HuckNature—Thematic connections to love of nature or American Romanticism
- #HuckFaith—Satirical scenes calling into question superstitions or religious beliefs

Feel free to hop on over to Twitter to check out any of these topics. And if you're planning a Twitter unit of your own, you are absolutely welcome to join in with my classes at any time. Or if you'd prefer to keep things small to start, using common hashtags across multiple teachers of the same course in your building is a fantastic way to get your "tribe" talking about the unit with their peers in other class sections!

Crazy high levels of student engagement. Instant content for a weekly class newsletter. And it doesn't feel the least bit like homework.

Best. Homework. Ever.

Since the assignment is framed more like a "choose your own adventure" than a linear question set, students find themselves looking more closely into the assigned text. If this were a Tough Mudder, they'd be helping one another climb on each other's shoulders to get over a wall, or throwing an arm out to help a buddy make their way up a particularly slippery hill. And with Twitter's hashtags, I find students genuinely get excited to lean on their "tribe" mates across class sections as they strike up conversations about their favorite findings and crowdsource answers for the biggest areas of confusion.

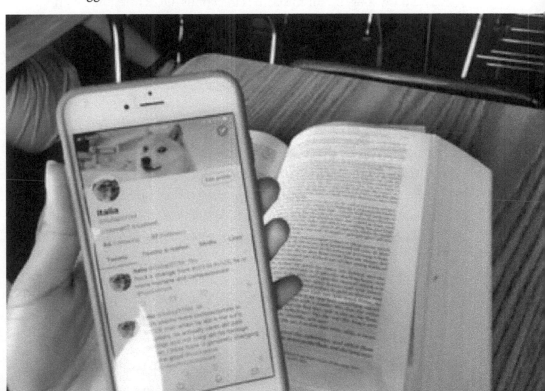

Best of all, my kids actually go home *and talk to their families (!!!)* about the work that we're covering in class. That's no small feat from the notoriously "too cool for school" teenage crowd. We're talking the kind of homework that inspires parents to send emails like this:

> I just thought you should know that last night (my son) exclaimed, 'This is the best homework I've ever had!' He was so motivated by the way you had the students annotate Huckleberry Finn.

And this:

> Our son has been ignited. He's writing. He's thinking. He's listening. He's interested. He TALKS ABOUT CLASS. So—we're grateful. And whether our son passes or fails your class, we're grateful for this turning point in his growth as a soon-to-be-man in a complicated world.

I'll say it again: Enthusiasm is infectious. OCRs are lined with cheering spectators that push competitors to be their absolute best. And Twitter is a brilliant tool for student engagement beyond the four walls of your classroom because it gives every single person a voice and the platform to express themselves for their entire team to hear.

Teaching, like endurance racing, draws strength from relationships. My fondest memories of OCRs haven't just been pushing myself through the crazy challenges—it's the fact that I've had the opportunity to conquer the courses with some of my closest friends and family members. Crushing the New York City Tough Mudder with my Boston Marathon qualifying cousin, Marianna, as she whipped through obstacles at lightning speed. Getting slung over my brother Jeremy's shoulders with our faces painted like professional wrestlers for the Wounded Warrior Carry in Virginia.

Barely keeping pace ahead of the sweeper car with my mom as she completed her first half marathon at age fifty-nine. Hopping on a roller coaster with my wife, Laura, at the halfway mark of the Walt Disney World Marathon.

Working together as a team of runners, we've learned how to read one another's body language, spotting even the slightest sign of a limp here, a hydration issue there, or the need for a moment's respite to catch our breaths before we tackle the next challenge. Our communication is stronger: We know which obstacle presents particular challenges for individual team members and who needs to hear what words of encouragement and when. We trust one another implicitly. And we're so much stronger together as a result.

Get in the Trenches

Worried that not every single student in every single class will catch the exact same information out of every single assigned page? Create a class Twitter account of your own and push out a handful of strategically timed tweets directed at entire classes or individual students to make sure they can get their eyes on the right portions of assignments before the next day's class. Suddenly you're more than just a spectator on the sidelines; you're right there in the trenches alongside them, offering positive feedback and support by firing off perfectly timed words of praise to help students see the progress they're making as they tackle any obstacles that your text provides. Pay it forward through your tribe by encouraging students to strike up peer-to-peer conversations by "liking" and retweeting one another's efforts. Start each new class day off with a five-minute Twitter highlight reel where you spotlight individual students whose tweets are really helping to propel your online discussion in the right direction. Just like an Obstacle

Course Race, it feels super satisfying to see photographic evidence of all your hard work!

"But how do I grade all this?"

If you're still working in a school system where creativity is encouraged but nightly homework grades are a necessary hazard of the job, set a simple quota for a minimum number of quality tweets per night per student. Mud runs and marathons let digital timing chips automatically keep track of the nitty gritty, so runners can focus only on the challenges at hand. If you'd prefer to let the magic of the internet do most of the heavy lifting for your classroom, set up individual "recipes" using If This Then That (ifttt.com) to create web-based triggers for easier sorting.

> **Note:** If you've never used IFTTT before, it's a free and fancy way to connect any one web-enabled thing to any other web-enabled thing. Like "IF" the weather app calls for rain, "THEN" send me a text message that says "Don't forget your umbrella!" Or "IF" (Twitter account X) sends a new tweet, "THEN" automatically add the contents of that message into a new line on a Google Sheet.

Students can do the same thing from their own Twitter accounts and Google Drive logins, which makes searching all of their annotations a breeze when it comes time to write an essay at the conclusion of the unit.

When you return to class, don't be afraid to celebrate all the great things that you're seeing from your students on Twitter! Just like a fresh batch of mud-drenched Tough Mudder photos—consider the instant jolt of social media adrenaline that a class can experience from:

- Using a tweet visualizer like TweetBeam.com or Twitterfall.com to make students feel like they've got a front row seat at a swank Silicon Valley tech conference.
- Firing up a tweet dashboard like TweetDeck.com or Hootsuite.com to keep tabs on multiple hashtagged conversations at the same time. (Note: Both of these sites are equally clutch for pre-scheduling questions for an in-class Twitter chat on a date when you know in advance that you'll be out of the building and need sub coverage.)
- Go inside the numbers with Twitonomy.com to provide easy-to-read visual breakdowns of each user's Twitter hashtag preferences, peer-to-peer connections, and patterns of behavior by frequency of interaction and time of day spent tweeting. And just like that, you've got a ready-made mini-lesson on our not-so-muddy digital footprint.

No Twitter, No Problems

Making student learning visible through Twitter is one of the many ways that social media can enhance your instructional practice and help students escape the usual homework slog of yet another Scantron quiz or reading compliance check worksheet. But if you're teaching younger students or your school or district still has restrictions on social media, there are plenty of alternatives. Regardless of the annotation format you use, keep in mind that it is critical to have students listen back to their own submissions after they're done. To echo George Couros in *The Innovator's Mindset*, "John Dewey once said, 'We do not learn from experience; we learn from reflecting on experience.' Reflection time should not be an optional component of the classroom or even done 'on your own time.' It should be a regular part of both student and educator practice."

Below are a handful of great tech tools that can help empower your tribe to grow and strengthen their learning together even if you're not able to use Twitter, adding instant #EDrenaline to break the everyday academic monotony.

Collaborative Comments

Cut and paste any assigned text into a Google Doc and grant your students shared "comment" access to strike up in-document annotations, comments, and conversations within the confines of a closed network.

Shared Annotations

Upload a .pdf of any document to KamiHQ.com, which syncs to your Google account, and anyone with the link can make annotations to a shared document.

Mind Maps

Hop on over to Coggle.com—another friendly one-stop shop with a Google login—to let your students splay their thoughts out on the page with interactive mind maps. You can even give multiple users the ability to edit and create inside the same master document.

VoiceThread

Upload any .pdf to a shared web space on VoiceThread.com, and students have the ability to add written comments, voice memos, or NFL commentator-style telestrator video annotations on the shared document for everyone to see.

Podcasts

If you have a smartphone, you can make a podcast. Just fire up the voice memo app and hit the big red button. No fancy sound

equipment required. And no additional software to install. Save the sound file to your Google Drive when you're done recording and send a link out to your podcasters to reflect on how they thought they fared.

Divide your class into student teams of four to six and scatter off to various corners of your classroom (or if you've got a longer timetable to work with, have them work together outside of school). Set an overhead timer for fifteen minutes and let groups record a miniature Socratic Seminar among themselves, in which they respond to a guided question set or simply pretend like they are a panel of experts being interviewed about [subject area X] on a late-night talk show. If you need to throw them a lifeline, consider sitting in as the "host" of the show, acting as conversation facilitator and helping to ensure that the ball keeps rolling for the entire duration of the recording session. After all, there's nothing worse in radio than dead air.

With collegial banter and good text evidence serving as the only two "rules" of a roundtable podcast, you can help your students develop closer bonds of trust and communication to make incredible strides towards supporting one another as a tribe. Just like good Mudders help their fellow competitors overcome any obstacle that the course throws their way, podcasts help students develop empathy, teamwork, and stronger communication skills as a direct result of working together to overcome these regularly scheduled challenges. If you'd like to check out samples from my classroom, head to iTunes and search for "DJO Round Table."

Flipgrid

If you haven't yet discovered Flipgrid, it's a blast. Free since the summer of 2018, Flipgrid creates a threaded discussion portal where students can use any device with a camera and a working internet connection (e.g., phones, tablets, laptops) to record and share short video responses directly from their devices. Once the videos have been uploaded, everything is neatly organized into a discussion-specific dashboard "grid." Students can click on one another's submissions in order to review the videos by their peers. Teachers and students can also post written and video responses on each video in the grid.

YouTube Meets EdPuzzle

If you prefer to stick to a more familiar video sharing web service, YouTube videos work just as well as those uploaded to Flipgrid. But one of my favorite dynamic duos for student-centered app-smashing is to ask students to find or upload their very own original content on YouTube, then sign up for a teacher account on EdPuzzle, so they can embed pop-up questions and production notes directly inside their YouTube creations for a self-reflective meta-assignment. You can even use a previous year's student-created videos to help pre-teach, re-teach, or assess the exact same content to a new tribe the following year.

Empower your students to become teachers through choice and voice. It is so important to celebrate successes and let students know that we see the hard work that they've put in! Every time I'm out in public and I see someone wearing a Spartan Race or Tough Mudder finisher T-shirt, I make sure to give them a quiet nod of respect to let them know that I see the mark of their accomplishment and that I'm impressed. Using EdPuzzle with YouTube for a one-two punch of mastery is a great way to let students see that their efforts haven't gone unnoticed. They've "been there, done that, got the T-shirt," and they've earned a powerful but silent measure of respect as part of the tribe.

Voxer and Marco Polo

If video isn't your thing but you're still looking to encourage social interaction and peer-to-peer networking, there's nothing better than having a digital walkie talkie where your "runners" can connect with the "course organizer" on demand. Steel sharpens steel, and free smartphone apps like Voxer or Marco Polo are a great way to get a team on the same page.

Voxer, Marco Polo, and many apps like them work like a digital walkie-talkie. With the push of a button, you can save, send, and stream a video or voice recording to anyone in the world. And both apps share a Netflix-like system of comprehensive message archives, which can be binge streamed for weeks after they've been recorded, creating a perfect "one stop shop" for content when looking back over a brain dump for large chunks of information at a time.

My wife, Laura, is a devoted music teacher. Her students use Voxer to record their voice parts and send them to her as miniature one-on-one singing quizzes. She's able to see exactly where each student is in terms of their own rehearsal progression, and she can fire back a quick recording to help point individual students in the right direction of how to improve. That's like having a personal trainer right there beside you, giving instant feedback as you complete your training runs! Not only is this expert scaffolding, but this free-flowing nature of the conversations helps students escape the antiquated notion that "learning" means every single person has to learn the exact same thing in the exact same way at the exact same time.

Questions for Discussion

1. Does your school allow students to have access to social media sites like Twitter? If not, could you use Google Docs or one of the other apps listed to add a social element to nightly homework? What other ways could you use social media or freeware in your classroom to help students feel connected to the fellow members of their "tribe" of learners as they work together to tackle the obstacles in your course's content?

2. Could your students become classroom co-teachers with a one-two punch of YouTube and EdPuzzle? Which units might lend themselves to this sort of activity?

3. How might you leverage social media to move from "sideline spectator" to "mud-covered runner in the trenches" while students tackle the obstacles of your course content? Is there a way to get your hands dirty and offer on-the-spot feedback beyond traditional grades?

PART III:

Escape Rooms

They who dream by day are cognizant of many things which escape those who dream only by night.

—Edgar Allan Poe, "Eleonora"

Chapter 7

Crafting High-Energy Class Escape Rooms

Scenario: It's a Friday night in Any City, USA. You and some friends are looking for a change of pace from the usual routine of dinner and a movie. Maybe laser tag or bowling? Nope. Brian reminds you that we're not sixteen anymore, and your buddy Raul has a weird thing about wearing other people's shoes. A board game? Forget it. Mike has a notoriously short attention span, and a three-hour round of Monopoly almost always ends in a fight.

With a mischievous smile, you say, "Hey, want to check out an Escape Room?"

And with that, you and a half dozen of your closest friends (or total strangers) pay *actual money* for the opportunity to get locked inside of an elaborately themed series of chambers in a high-stakes race against the clock. Can you survive a teeming horde of zombies? Decode ancient hieroglyphics? Disarm the nuclear codes that will save the world from World War III? Suddenly, you're not just watching an adventure: You're *living* it! Pulse pounding with all the adrenaline of an action-packed blockbuster, your brain's pleasure centers flood with dopamine as you crack code after code to bring your crew one step closer to a thrilling escape from this living Rubik's Cube. For the next sixty minutes, it's you and your buddies working side by side through a series of high-stakes puzzles and challenges in a race to unlock the pharaoh's treasure, decipher the clues of an alien planet, or rescue the sunken treasure of Atlantis.

No athletic ability is required, and no time is spent "on the bench" watching other people play while waiting for your turn.

In teacher speak, this is total engagement.

Building Your First Escape Room

Whether you're using physical clues or designing your own custom escape room scenario with Google Forms, there is a bit of a learning curve when it comes to figuring out how, exactly, to design a class escape room. We'll get into the nitty gritty and the theatrics in just a bit, but for anyone who's looking to try their hand at this game-changing approach to lesson design, I've found it helpful to break class escape room design into three basic principles:

1. Feelings Come First

In *Actionable Gamification: Beyond Points, Badges, and Leaderboards*, gamification pioneer Yu-Kai Chou emphasizes the critical importance of putting the desired feelings of a target gamer before the desired behaviors. I'll let him explain:

> Instead of starting with what game elements and game mechanics to use, the good game designer may begin by thinking, *Okay, how do I want my users to feel? Do I want them to feel inspired? Do I want them to feel proud? Should they be scared? Anxious? What's my goal for their intended experience?*

Once the designer understands how she wants her users to feel, then she begins to think, *Okay, what kind of game elements and mechanics can help me accomplish my goals of ensuring players feel this way*? The solution may lie in swords, plants, or perhaps word puzzles, but the whole point here is that game elements are just a means to an end, instead of an end in itself. Game elements are simply there to push and pull on their users' behavioral core drives.

If you're a literature teacher, you may need students to solve a puzzle related to vocabulary. If you're a math teacher, your class might need to memorize fractions. But simply handing your students a vocab puzzle and saying, "Solve all of these problems to save character (x)" probably won't set their world on fire. Feelings come first! And each puzzle should help the student feel like they're taking one step closer to a major breakthrough. Divide the main narrative across four or five separate puzzle-solving stations, and every student will feel like they're making a meaningful contribution towards the greater goal.

An example:

Feelings Come First

"Atticus Finch is in trouble, and it looks like the angry mob has bad intentions (dread)! But poor Scout is stuck in detention with a pop quiz (frustration) from Miss Caroline. Help Scout score a perfect exam on her assignment (pride), so you can race to her father's side (heroism) before it's too late. And watch out for the vengeful Bob Ewell (pressure), who is hot on your tail!"

Escape Room Tasks

- Ace Miss Caroline's Exam by completing a fill-in-the-blank worksheet.

- Escape The Classroom by following a scavenger hunt with themed clues.
- Avoid Bob Ewell by correctly identifying which events happened where.
- Disperse the Mob by correctly identifying a series of character quote ID questions.
- Rescue Atticus by sorting the events of the novel into a timeline.

Empathy is essential in the classroom, and a well-crafted narrative helps any escape room spring to life with opportunities for our students to see the world through the eyes of the heroes of our course content.

2. Embrace a Theme

Will your students be rescuing a character from peril? Trying to locate a series of scrambled clues in order to solve a *Da Vinci Code* style mystery? Maybe they are a team of post-apocalyptic survivalists, using advanced concepts in math or science classrooms to help defend the future of the human race! You can use any theme or content area that you'd like, but the success of your escape room lives and dies by the strength of the narrative behind it.

Whatever your theme is, choose it early and use it as the lifeblood to drive the theming of your high-stakes escape room. Everything that your scenario contains—puzzles, characters, clues, secrets, artifacts—will proceed from there. It helps if your theme has non-academic application and connects into something that can genuinely spark the interest of a child. Spotting grammar mistakes or solving math problems before time runs out isn't nearly as fun as cracking secret codes to escape an alien planet or launch an intergalactic space shuttle and save the universe (even if it is the exact same set of problems). A compelling story is everything!

3. Keys and Chambers

Sometimes puzzles will need to be solved in a particular order so that one chamber unlocks a hidden clue or a secret key to help you solve another. But more often than not—especially in cases where you have entire classrooms of student groups working asynchronously—it pays to have most tasks feel like they're a stand-alone "key" that helps tie back to the larger narrative. Incremental victories help a class sustain momentum and build excitement as precious seconds tick away on the overhead clock. Too many victories can make the scenario feel too easy, but no signs of progress for a full sixty minutes can make the experience feel like little more than a gussied-up worksheet.

For example, let's say you are a Spanish class. Your escape room scenario throws your students into the center of the *Plaza de Toros*, where they're staring into the eyes of an angry bull ready to charge! You've only got sixty minutes of stamina up your sleeve, and you'll need to solve five separate puzzles in order to make your escape.

Feelings Come First

The order in which the individual puzzles are solved doesn't really matter in this scenario. It's a simple game of beat the clock. That means pressure will rise, and the bullfight will continue until the very last "lock" is opened, so you'll need to create puzzles that offer some sense of mounting accomplishment as the countdown clock ticks closer and closer to a thrilling escape.

Embrace a Theme

This escape room will plunge your students into the bullfight arena, so start thinking about all of the characters, items, and setting details that they'd likely encounter in that space. Seasoned matadors, charging bulls, colorful outfits, and cheering crowds are a must. Fire up a quick YouTube playlist of "Bullfight Arena Music," and you've got a ready-made escape room soundtrack!

Keys and Chambers

Perhaps one puzzle could help students earn a red cape, while a second puzzle sees them obtain a *Traje de Luces* (the bullfighter's sequined suit), and a third earns them some sort of trumpet to momentarily distract the charging beast's attention, while a fourth puzzle snags them the assistance of a professional *picador* to buy you some time, and a fifth puzzle, which can only be solved using clues obtained from each of the other four puzzles, ultimately scores them a rope ladder to make a daring last second escape.

Much like the Disney-inspired design ideas from Chapter 1, your *Plaza de Toros* escape room is packed with an innate sense of story, place, and purpose. And the logical extensions of this fantasy scenario might ask students to translate words, numbers, and phrases on different "event posters" or "newspaper articles" to discover the rich history and cultural controversy surrounding these events as they help their heroic bullfighter escape the ring.

Even better, in about as much time as it might have otherwise taken you to make a worksheet, you will have created an in-house "field trip" that can spark memories to last a lifetime.

Though escape rooms can also be used as a pre-teaching tool at the start of a brand new unit, I've personally found them to be of greatest impact when used as a test for mastery at the conclusion of a longer unit of study. Since everyone in your class will have spent two or three weeks studying the same content, a summative assessment is a perfect time to convert just about any traditional end-of-unit exam into a full-blown escape room.

The easiest way to do this is to look at the transfer skills that you are currently testing for at the conclusion of your unit. Grant Wiggins and Jay McTighe's "Backwards Design" model points out that your average three-week unit typically focuses on three to five different skills that the students will carry with them after that particular unit of study has ended. Five skills equal five puzzles, and each puzzle can focus specifically on one of those skills.

Once you've decided on a theme, look closely at the printed format of your existing assessment as it appears on the page. Is it divided into a "part one," "part two," and "part three" style breakdown, testing for multiple skills over the course of the printed assessment? If so, you just saved yourself a ton of work in your puzzle design.

Take your average humanities exam:

- Questions relating to key dates or historical figures can be turned into a timeline puzzle. Fill in all of the missing event dates (in the correct order!) to unlock the secret code.

- Questions relating to identifying major civilizations or landmasses and geography can be turned into a map puzzle. Sort each event into the place where it happened (maybe with a certain point value at each geographical location?) and you'll solve the puzzle.

When you're through exploring, place all answers in number order from greatest to least according to the number that each contains. Use only the top-scoring numbers in sequence to open the lock.

- Questions relating to conflicting ideologies or political theories (or different components of a Venn diagram or taxonomy) can be turned into a sorting puzzle.

TWO HOUSEHOLDS

"Two households, both alike in dignity..."
- Prince, Act I, Scene I

The ancient grudge has broken forth a new mutiny! And civil blood is promising to make civil hands unclean unless you can step in and sort this heated rivalry out.

Can you divide the lines spoken between the respective households from which they came?

To settle this dispute, take your time with the eyewitness testimonies provided. Then take the total points scored by the Montagues and subtract it from the total points scored by the Capulets.

Montague

HOUSE
OF
CAPULET

Suspect name:
Balthasar

Time of interview:
4:49 p.m.

Quote:
"Look man, yeah, I was there. But they started it! Abram and I were just minding our own business."

Suspect name:
Abram

Time of interview:
4:52 p.m.

Quote:
"Don't ask me, pal. We're not the ones biting our thumbs at strangers in the streets! Ask Balthasar, he'll tell you. We're clean!!"

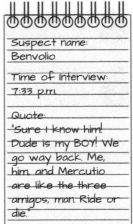

Suspect name:
Benvolio

Time of interview:
7:33 p.m.

Quote:
"Sure I know him! Dude is my BOY! We go way back. Me, him, and Mercutio are like the three amigos, man. Ride or die."

- Questions relating to specific text or document-based details can be turned into puzzles testing close reading skills.

TRYING TO START AMERICA'S BANK

"ELIZA, I'VE GOT SO MUCH ON MY PLATE!"

HELP HAMILTON MAKE SENSE OF THE NUMBERS THAT KEEP PILING UP AROUND HIM. YOU'LL NEED THE TOTAL SUM OF ALL 24 CLUES. BUT NO CALCULATORS ALLOWED! SO PICK UP A PEN AND START WRITING.

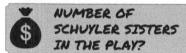

NUMBER OF DUEL COMMANDMENTS?

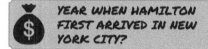

YEAR WHEN HAMILTON FIRST ARRIVED IN NEW YORK CITY?

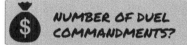

NUMBER OF SCHUYLER SISTERS IN THE PLAY?

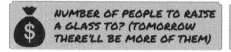

NUMBER OF PEOPLE TO RAISE A GLASS TO? (TOMORROW THERE'LL BE MORE OF THEM)

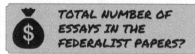

DEGREES OF HEAT DURING THE BATTLE OF MONMOUTH?

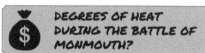

TOTAL NUMBER OF ESSAYS IN THE FEDERALIST PAPERS?

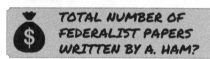

TOTAL NUMBER OF FEDERALIST PAPERS WRITTEN BY A. HAM?

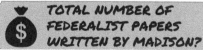

TOTAL NUMBER OF FEDERALIST PAPERS WRITTEN BY MADISON?

- Questions relating to unit vocabulary can quickly be turned into a crossword puzzle. (Use a free crossword puzzle generator like Flippity.net) Circle certain squares or letters in the puzzle and have students fill in each of the missing items in order to parse out a secret password.

Across

3. growth mindset opinion towards others success
6. sweet old school extrinsic motivation
7. intrinsic motivator, or something personal and small you'd carry
10. Lewis and Virginia Eaton Professor of Psychology at Stanford University
13. fixed mindset opinion towards others success
15. Charlie Sheen catch phrase, extrinsic goal
16. fixed mindset attitude towards effort
17. fixed mindset reaction towards criticism
20. intrinsic motivator, like George the little monkey
21. classic extrinsic motivator tandem
23. extrinsic motivators at work or in career paths
24. growth mindset attitude towards obstacles

Down

1. Extrinsic motivators for show, like the scouts
2. First of three "Beyond" elements, according to Yu Kai Chou
4. "Why should I bother?" opposite
5. intrinsic motivation, like reason for playing a game
8. Giant-sized tallies of winners and losers
9. fixed mindset attitude towards obstacles
11. Intrinsic motivator of Fleetwood Mac's "You can go your own way!"
12. fixed mindset attitude towards challenges
14. growth mindset attitude towards effort
18. growth mindset reaction towards criticism
19. growth mindset attitude towards challenges
22. sticky old school extrinsic motivators

EXHIBIT F

- "Who said what" and true or false questions make for an easy sorting puzzle, where the exact code to open the lock could be designed such that students need to correctly identify the exact numeric totals for EVERY single prompt.

- If you want students to focus on a passage or problem where errors have been strategically embedded somewhere in the formula or response, you can use the same approach for an easy puzzle design ("Count the mistakes in a problem" or "Add up the point total for all of the numbered examples that contain wrong answers").

"The technological revolution is not going to go away. Students are used to the ability to connect to each other and have access to information at all times. We can either fight against this irrepressible force, or we can choose to use it." #tlap

— @BurgessDave

"Standing out from the crowd is the only way to guarantee your message is received in a culture that is increasingly distracted and where attention spans are plummeting."

— Teach Like a Pirate

"I would much rather my kids leave my class with the strength of character and courage to fight racism when they find it, than have memorized some facts about the Civil Rights Act of 1964. I'm not saying you can't have both, I'm just pointing out that only one of those things will be measured on the test — and it isn't the most important one."

— @BurgessDave

- Scavenger hunts are a great way to test for close reading while introducing a little bit of kinesthetic activity to your escape room. Scatter a series of clues at strategic locations throughout your classroom, with key words in each clue (or even highlighted in UV ink) to point searchers in the direction of the next clue in the series.

CLUE #1

WILLY: I don't want a change! I want Swiss cheese. Why am I always being contradicted?

LINDA *(with a covering laugh)*: I thought it would be a surprise.

WILLY: Why don't you open a window in here, for God's sake?

CLUE #2

BIFF: I am not a leader of men, Willy, and neither are you. You were never anything but a hard-working drummer who landed in the ash can like all the rest of them!

- A scavenger hunt puzzle can even culminate in a brain teaser or closed-response question prompt where students will need to demonstrate the single, correct answer in order to receive a key.

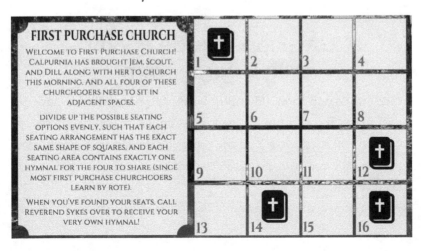

FIRST PURCHASE CHURCH

WELCOME TO FIRST PURCHASE CHURCH! CALPURNIA HAS BROUGHT JEM, SCOUT, AND DILL ALONG WITH HER TO CHURCH THIS MORNING. AND ALL FOUR OF THESE CHURCHGOERS NEED TO SIT IN ADJACENT SPACES.

DIVIDE UP THE POSSIBLE SEATING OPTIONS EVENLY, SUCH THAT EACH SEATING ARRANGEMENT HAS THE EXACT SAME SHAPE OF SQUARES, AND EACH SEATING AREA CONTAINS EXACTLY ONE HYMNAL FOR THE FOUR TO SHARE (SINCE MOST FIRST PURCHASE CHURCHGOERS LEARN BY ROTE).

WHEN YOU'VE FOUND YOUR SEATS, CALL REVEREND SYKES OVER TO RECEIVE YOUR VERY OWN HYMNAL!

- Augmented Reality (AR) puzzles, or red lens decoder clues, are perfect for an instant shot of #EDrenaline in any content area. Use free AR apps like HP Reveal, Metaverse, Blippar, and QR codes to embed an invisible, scannable element directly inside of any printed material.

Low-Prep Escape Rooms with Google Forms

Here's the good news: Planning an escape room doesn't have to cost you a ton of time, money, or supplies. If you can create a Google Form, you've got all the tools you'll need for a super low-prep escape room in no more time than it takes to create your average worksheet.

Let's start with the basics.

Google Forms gives users the ability to create password-protected questions using what's known as the "Response Validation" feature. It's a little-known form builder's trick that can be found by clicking the three dots in the bottom right-hand corner of any question on a Google Form. With response validation enabled, you'll turn any question into a sort of response-protected prompt item, kind of like those online shopping sites that force you to enter your credit card's three-digit CVV code before they'll let you make a purchase. Whether your students are answering questions about key dates from a historical timeline or solving square roots to help repair the mainframe of a stranded rocket ship, the digital "locks" won't open until every single keystroke is correct. This is especially handy when writing a question prompt that asks for a particularly important number or the exact spelling of a super-top-secret password.

If you're looking to up the ante for a more challenging escape room, you can stack a bunch of these "secret password" style questions together on a single page Google Form, so users have to provide the *exact information required for each question* before the form will allow them to proceed. Since the form simply won't allow anyone to submit it without getting every single question item exactly correct, it's a perfect way to let the tech do the heavy lifting for you and draw attention to specific vocabulary words or number-based solutions.

Got the basics? Rock on! This simple one-step process is all you need to go live with a basic escape room, which lends itself beautifully to any content area questions or themed scenario of your choice. Simply share the link to the Google Form with your students, set a countdown timer (and maybe play some dramatic music) on the overhead projector, and your escape room is off to the races.

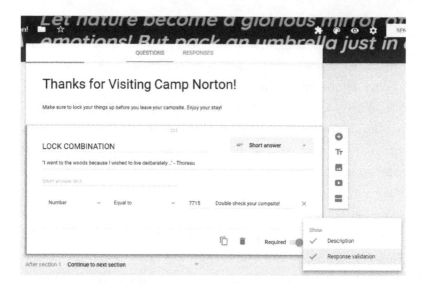

But if you're looking to take your escape room drama beyond the basics, then you're in luck! There are a bunch of clever features in Google Forms that will help you add twists and turns into your escape room to really heighten the suspense and difficulty of the activity.

"Timed Lock" Doors with Length Validation

The CVV code is a frustrating stopgap, to be sure. But it's a perfect way to make sure that you've entered all of the necessary information. You can use this same approach to make sure that students are taking their writing submissions seriously as they make their way through a password-protected Google Form. The Response Validation feature also gives form builders the option to create a rule that won't allow anyone to submit their answer to a particular prompt unless they type a certain number of characters. And while sheer length and overall strength of a student response are not necessarily correlated, there's still plenty of fun to be had by posing certain questions that require a response of no less than (x) characters—as the length validation will force your students to continue providing additional details and paying closer attention to a particular prompt question before hastily clicking the "submit" button.

Even if you're not sure that a full-blown escape room is quite your style just yet, you can absolutely use a single, length-validated Google Form question prompt as a daily warm-up or exit ticket collection tool. And as your students develop their timed writing abilities throughout the year, you can keep raising the threshold of required characters that they must type before the form will allow them to submit their responses!

Multiple-Choice Questions and "Dead Ends"

Perhaps my all-time favorite Google Form escape room curveball is the almighty "dead end" trick, which sends students spiraling back to an earlier page in the form (or way back to the very start of the form altogether!) if they get a single answer wrong. Think of the endless maze of The Lost Woods from *The Legend of Zelda*: one false step, untold hours of frustration.

The good news for us humans is that computers (like old-school combination locks) only think in binary. Right answer? Go here. Wrong answer? Go there. And multiple choice items in Google Forms have the power to do the same thing. Check out a sample of this multi-stage Google Form escape room at EDrenalineRush.com/Resources then come back here for an easy-to-follow recipe of how the sausage is made:

1. Create a Google Form with at least two sections by clicking the "ADD SECTION" menu option. (It's the double-decker icon located at the bottom of the menu just to the right of the question.)

2. Put a multiple-choice question on section one of the form and click the Response Validation feature to say, "Go to section based on answer." You can now set your response

validation so that the form will automatically direct users to different sections of the form based on the answer that they submit.

3. If the correct answer is selected, the form will automatically take users to the next section where they can continue answering questions and solving whatever secrets might await them inside. But . . .

4. If the incorrect answer is selected, the form can be set to take users down a dead-end path or boot them back to the start of their journey with no choice but to begin the entire process again from stage one.

My favorite way to add complexity to a multi-stage Google Form escape room is to mix-and-match these different lock styles together in a domino-like series across multiple sections of the form. Create a form with just one or two questions per page, which gives students the feeling that they're progressing through a series of "chambers" in a real-life escape room. This gives students a mounting sense of confidence as they pass through two or three

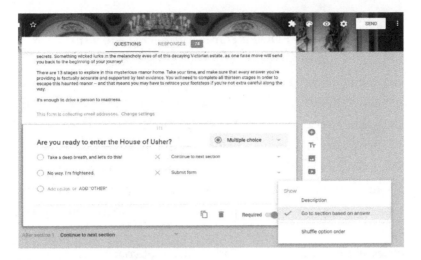

stages in a row using password-protected locks. It then heightens the suspense by throwing in a "timed" lock with a length-validated response or multiple-choice question that has the power to send them right back to the beginning of their journey if they get it wrong.

Next-Level Escape Rooms with Breakout EDU

Google Forms are fun, but the adrenaline rush of a real-life escape room lies in the kinesthetic thrill of hands-on discovery, like using UV flashlights to illuminate hidden secrets written in invisible ink, chasing down a series of clues in a real-life scavenger hunt, stumbling upon a physical key, or feeling the joyous metal "click" of a combination lock as it opens in your hand.

Enter Breakout EDU.

In 2015, two teachers named James Sanders and Mark Hammons created an education startup company called Breakout EDU, offering tangible classroom kits that captured the high-energy spirit of real-life escape rooms while testing "The Four C's" of critical thinking, collaboration, creativity, and cooperation. The $150 Breakout EDU kit comes with a large and a small box, a locking hasp with five physical locks (four resettable combination locks and one with an actual key), a UV ink pen, a UV flashlight, a miniature thumb drive, a red decoder lens, and a deck of reflection cards for the group to discuss and digest after the timed escape room scenario has ended. Included in the price, you'll also get a full year's subscription to their electronic portal with more than 300 different plug-and-play escape room scenarios for all sorts of subjects and grade levels. Best of all, if the site doesn't have a scenario that fits your content area, you can even adapt existing templates and tailor them to the unique needs of your class.

If you're serious about class escape room design, it's a steal.

In the first class escape room I created, my students became travelers in the 1800s, passing through the sleepy town of Concord, Massachusetts, when they'd discover that the famed thinker Henry David Thoreau had been thrown into jail following a political protest. The goal was for students to use their knowledge of 1800s rhetoric and poetry and distract the guards long enough to break the locks and help this transcendental genius escape to the nearby retreat of Walden Pond. And in the radical spirit of the free-thinking American Romantics, the plan was to use this collaborative class-wide activity in place of our regularly scheduled end-of-unit exam.

We had ten days to prepare for our first-ever class escape room. Now it was time to start selling the drama.

The Impresario with a Scenario

In *Teaching as the Art of Staging*, Elon University Professor Anthony Weston traces the evolution of teaching through the traditional "sage on the stage" model of nonstop teacher talk through the more contemporary "guide on the side" approach, where educators serve in a role more like that of a coach or facilitator. But as Dr. Weston sees it, there's an even more potent secret weapon in any teacher's toolbox.

Become "The Impresario with a Scenario."

As Weston explains, the primary work of the teacher is to put students into an urgently engaging and self-unfolding scenario, trusting the learners to carry it forward, while preparing to join in as needed. In the days leading up to our dramatic reveal, full-color photographs of Walden Pond and a giant message of "#ESCAPE" would "randomly" appear in our slideshow. With each interruption, I'd pretend like the presentation software was acting up, as I quickly fiddled with the remote and went on with the regularly scheduled program.

Then I used a free app to create a lightning-fast .gif of photos excerpted from our current unit of study, with the word #ESCAPE flashing over the top of Romantic icon images like Edgar Allan Poe, Ralph Waldo Emerson, and Henry David Thoreau. Using Remind.com, students received text messages containing these animated montages with zero explanation.

My class Twitter feed was commandeered by The Concord Police Department with all-points bulletins issued for officers to be on the lookout for one Henry David Thoreau.

Our escape room had already begun.

When Thursday morning arrived, I had twenty-four excited students lined up at the classroom door, buzzing with curiosity to make sense of just what, exactly, this whole #ESCAPE thing could be all about. They were greeted by an ominous sign over the window on my door.

DO NOT ENTER. THE PRISONER IS BEING TAKEN INTO CUSTODY.
—Concord Police Department

As I scrambled inside the classroom to lay out the finishing touches on a series of themed puzzles, I could hear the energy resonating through the doorway as students were buzzing with questions and conspiracy theories.

"Who's the prisoner? Are WE the prisoners!?"

"What is Mr. Meehan doing in there?! He's up to something!"

"Wait—are we going on a class trip?"

Three… two… one.

I opened the door, and twenty-four faces turned to me, all dead silent, their eyes locked on me in rapt attention, awaiting further instruction and hanging on to every word that I could possibly think to say. So I cleared my throat dramatically and mustered my best "authority" voice:

"Make your way into the facility. Do not touch any of the evidence you see before you. Remain standing and await further instructions."

As the students entered the classroom, they caught glimpses of brightly colored puzzles and clues scattered on desks and bookshelves around the room. They could not help but notice the giant black box positioned on a desk at the front of the classroom, menacingly held shut by half a dozen physical locks and a large metal hasp. Once everyone made their way into the classroom, I queued up a quick iMovie hype trailer video on the overhead screen, and our simulation was underway!

Unlikely Classroom Heroes

My school offers an expanded services program for students with moderate intellectual or cognitive delays. In our student body of just over 1,100, we have about ten students in the building who receive these services, working closely with student mentors for inclusion classes as they take part in non-degree-seeking courses.

It is an amazing witness to the dignity of the human person to see students of all ability levels working together in classrooms throughout our school, and, even though our students who receive expanded services complete a modified curriculum, seeing them included in college prep and honors-level classes throughout the building does a lot of good for every individual involved.

Eight minutes into our first escape room scenario, the class was starting to find themselves frustrated. Here we had a room full of honors students who had long become savvy at how to "play the game of school" and deliver back exactly what a teacher had requested. But in the class escape room? Many of the same advanced level students started to feel the pressure. For more than a handful in this group of learners who were used to having things

come more easily to them, this escape room was quickly shaping up to be a dead end.

That's when Janie (not her real name), one of my students who receives expanded services and the support of a student mentor, made a game-changing discovery.

"The different puzzles are different colors!" she said with a smile.

Janie was exactly right. The puzzles were color-coded, but I had deliberately scrambled clues of different colors at random across the various desk groups throughout the room to throw the class for a loop. And while so many of her classmates became laser focused on trying to solve the particular set of puzzles that they had found on their own desk cluster, they'd missed the biggest clue of all! By pointing out the fact that different puzzles were printed on different colors of paper, Janie had cracked the first code.

Armed with Janie's eagle-eyed discovery, students quickly redistributed the color-coded puzzle pieces to various desk clusters

throughout the classroom. As the massive, overhead timer ticked closer to zero, one by one, the locks began to fall. Students were high-fiving one another as each new discovery was made. Progress gave rise to more progress as the class was able to get very real and immediate feedback that their efforts were inching them ever closer to springing the prisoner from his jail cell.

In the end, the escape room was a resounding success. We took the last five minutes of class to offer some written reflections on what we'd learned. Here's what Justin, one of my high school juniors, had to say:

"I felt that today's activity is literally perfect for the system of education that students have been talking about. It caused every single student to interact with one another while being attentive and learning. Teachers were here to give us a foundation or hints when we were stuck, but it was still us as a class that learned and had to talk to each other. This activity also made us think critically and manage our time, making it a more realistic scenario in our real lives. The puzzle I worked on the most was the salmon-colored one with the school schedule on it. It really caused me to think, and with the help of my other classmates, I eventually solved it. This was honestly the best activity I have done in any class."

We closed the activity by asking students to select MVP awards for the classmates they believed helped the group the most. Far and away, Janie was the unanimous choice as the star of our class, and you could see her face glowing with pride for weeks afterwards as her classmates constantly made a point of referencing back to her color-coded discovery.

Students Sound Off

When time expires in your escape room and students have either cracked the code or found themselves just a few tantalizing seconds away from solving all the clues, wrapping up the activity with a reflection exercise is a great way to hammer home the lessons of the day with some serious metacognition. Some questions you might consider including:

- What was your biggest success in today's escape room?
- What was your biggest struggle in today's escape room?
- Which classmate(s) really impressed you with their leadership and puzzle solving abilities?
- What particular skills did the puzzle(s) test you on? How could you have better prepared for this puzzle knowing what you know now?
- What advice would you give to a new student who was attempting to tackle a similar escape room for the very first time?

Note: There really is no greater feeling than having students ask for "five minutes more! Pleeeeease!"—and you're certainly welcome to provide it to them.

Once you get into the general groove of escape-inspired assessment design, you'll start to find that it actually flows just as quickly as writing a traditional exam (in some cases, even faster because you no longer have to dream up three or four wrong answers for every single correct answer). After you've tried a series of escape rooms and your classes have gotten the hang of how the activity can work, you can even turn the keys over to your students to transform your entire classroom into a massive Project Based Assessment escape room design makerspace! Now instead of taking a test, your students will be *making* one. And each class section can design their very own escape room puzzles that rival class sections (or future classes of students) will have to complete in order to wrap up the unit.

Questions for Discussion

1. Think of a current unit assessment that might lend itself to a themed class escape room. What would the exact same content and questions look like if they were presented as part of a cohesively themed puzzle scenario?

2. If staging a full-blown class escape room still feels daunting, is there a possible opportunity to use a password-protected Google Form to inject a sense of excitement to a one-off lesson?

3. Look at the unit of your curriculum that typically presents the lowest levels of student engagement. Is there an existing pop culture trend (zombies, *Fortnite*, superheroes) that you could borrow for an escape room scenario to give your content a fresh coat of paint?

Chapter 8

From Breakout to Break In—*Reverse* Escape Rooms

It is our choices, Harry, that show what we truly are, far more than our abilities.

—Albus Dumbledore, *Harry Potter and the Chamber of Secrets*

My students absolutely loved our class escape rooms, but these full-blown scenarios definitely took some time and theatrics to set up, and I was bugged by the fact that not every student ended up having access to every puzzle each time we ran the activities. Likewise, there's an inevitable logjam at the very end of most escape room activities when some 20+ students crowd around a table that's only so big to watch a handful of their peers try to bust open that final lock. So sure, this whole class approach was great for the end of a unit, but for breaking "in" to new content? Not so much.

Sometimes teachers just need to make sure that every single student is presented with the exact same information, which inevitably gives rise to time-tested pedagogy like stand and deliver lectures and whole group instruction. The only problem? Lectures don't work. Nobel Prize-winning physicist Dr. Carl Weimer once found that a mere 10 percent of students remembered the answer to a question taught via lecture just 20 minutes prior. And for all those dedicated teachers out there who supplement their lectures with PowerPoint, Prezi, or Google slideshows? Research suggests that we might just be wasting our time. In *Unmistakable Impact*, University of Kansas coaching institute director Jim Knight explains:

> *Everyone I know has sat through enough PowerPoint Presentations to know that the default PowerPoint format does not lead to clear communication. Nancy Duarte even reports that the men who created PowerPoint were quoted to the Wall Street Journal as saying, "The best way to paralyze an opposing army is to ship them PowerPoint" As Seth Godin in* Really Bad PowerPoint (and how to avoid) *nicely, but pretty directly, puts it: "PowerPoint is a dismal failure. Almost every PowerPoint presentation sucks rotten eggs."*

So what makes lectures and slideshows so ineffective? Cognitive overload. Much like a sponge trying to absorb water, the human brain can only process so much new information at the same time before it has to dump that load into more long-term storage and try again. Research is pretty consistent that most humans can only store about seven new items of information at a time. But when you're frantically taking notes from a slideshow full of images and bullet point items, it's like trying to drink from a firehose.

You can't absorb new information when your sponge is full.

A Better Mousetrap

Lectures fail because students are passive receptors in endless streams of information. Slideshows presuppose that students will raise their hands when they have questions, but those same learners—who are literally too overwhelmed with all the new information at once to realize that they are completely lost—are, in fact, the absolute *least* likely to seek help.

Escape rooms work because participants get instant feedback as they squeeze their mental sponges out in a repeating process of trial and error. The lock either opens, or it doesn't. Right answers propel you forward, and you are rewarded with new challenges. Wrong answers force you to double-check your thinking, review your notes, talk through the places where you're getting stuck, and try another solution. A good puzzle increases the challenge level as the game progresses. As Doug Lemov reminds us in his seminal classroom teacher's playbook *Teach Like a Champion:* "The reward for right answers . . . will be harder questions." Learning never stops.

What if you could pull off an Escape Room *in reverse*? What might it look like if the classroom could capture all the adrenaline and excitement of a traditional escape room, but the teacher could still guarantee each student's equal exposure to every single puzzle *and* collect a slew of bite-sized work products to prove individual concept mastery?

Enter #QRBreakIN.

At the outset, I envisioned #QRBreakIN as a sort of "reverse escape room," like a small group relay race through old-school

centers: all of the adrenaline, none of the time on the bench. While I was at it, I wanted to correct some issues I'd experienced when running a traditional stations activity (specifically, the age-old "3-2-1, rotate!" approach, when it's immediately clear that some groups might have been done for ages, while others are nowhere near ready to move on). Now, instead of working together as a class to break out, smaller student teams compete to break IN to a new unit of study, teaching themselves by solving asynchronous puzzles in a race against their peers and the clock. Hold up a minute—"teaching *themselves*"?

Yup. From Maria Montessori through *Minecraft*, there are scads of studies to suggest that students can actually learn *without* a teacher's direct intervention. In fact, an article in the January 12, 2009 issue of *Science Daily* cited findings from a team out of the University of Colorado Boulder who observed, "Even when students in a discussion group all got the initial answer wrong, after talking to each other they were able to figure out the correct response, to learn."

#QRBreakIN in 30 Seconds

A #QRBreakIN "reverse" escape room takes information that would otherwise have been delivered in a traditional lecture or slideshow and turns it into a team-based scavenger hunt-like race through a series of puzzle centers (or "chambers"). One concept is to have eight to twelve chambers, each of which can be explored in any order that a student team might like. Post a single class set of printed instruction slides (8 centers = 8 pages) and let teams loose, solving puzzles with one-to-one device access. The overhead board keeps track of a giant countdown clock and provides a scoreboard, tracking which teams have completed which chambers, keeping everyone motivated and working hard.

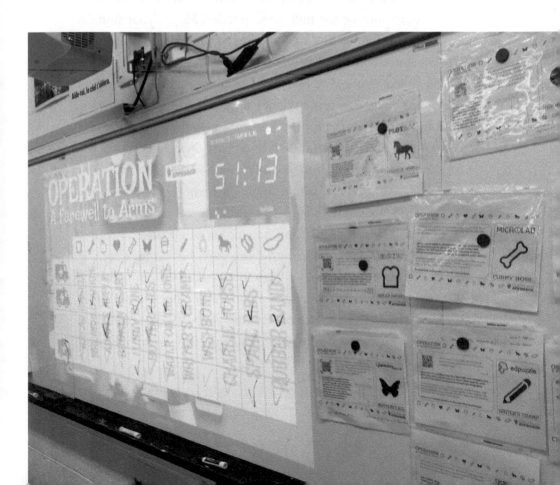

Building from what we know about cognitive load theory, for each chamber there's a corresponding work product. Grab an instruction sheet for the chamber of your choice and take it back to your desk group to solve as a team. Once you've entered a chamber, there's no going back! And that means your team is trapped working on that chamber's puzzle until you can deliver the work product to standard. Solve the puzzle and your team is free to make its way to another chamber of your choice to rinse and repeat the process. The first team to successfully complete all eight chambers wins the game. At that point, either the winning team can play a bonus level with enrichment activities, or all other groups can complete outstanding chambers for homework.

Like a traditional escape room, each #QRBreakIN starts with a cohesive theme to provide a broader sense of unity and a narrative through line for the individual puzzles. Maybe your unit on World War I unfolds like a giant game of *Risk*, where competing teams bounce between different "countries," solving themed puzzles to collect "troops" to bolster their ranks. Perhaps your study of *A Raisin in the Sun* sees student teams collecting puzzles to correspond with different property values to help the Younger family move out of Chicago's South Side and chase their dreams of starting a new life in the well-to-do, Boardwalk-like neighborhood of Clybourne Park. What if your unit on *The Great Gatsby* played like the classic whodunnit *Clue*, where player teams explore various "rooms" in a luxurious mansion, solving various puzzles to collect themed "artifacts" about the mysterious party host as they go?

There are limitless possibilities for themes you can use for a reverse escape room. I've posted a handful of template examples on EDrenalineRush.com/Resources that you're welcome to use as a jumping off point for inspiration. Click the dropdown file menu to save a copy and feel free to edit them to your liking!

Challenge Flags and Penalty Boxes

To keep your #QRBreakIN running smoothly, teachers will want to be free to roam about the classroom to spot-check work products and offer on-the-fly assistance. Even though student groups are problem-solving at their own pace, sometimes a team might need an extra bit of support along the way. For this reason, I always provide each team with two "challenge flags" that they can use any time they get totally stuck. Playing a challenge flag (just like an NFL coach) earns students the chance to call the teacher over to their group for more specific instructions or clarification on a particular puzzle. They only have two challenge flags to use throughout the duration of the game, so the team will need to work together to use them wisely, which helps them learn to clarify one another's questions as they go.

On the flipside, I also like to equip certain puzzles with "boobytraps." If a group calls the teacher over to review a particular work product and it's not up to snuff for any reason, the teacher

reserves the right to trigger the "penalty box." The group will be trapped in that center for two excruciating minutes to revise their work product and watch helplessly as other teams race ahead of them before they are allowed to call you over to check their work product again. This is also an excellent tool for on-the-fly scaffolding, as a teacher can offer additional support for groups needing direct instruction or ask clarifying enrichment questions (and slow down the pace!) of groups flying through puzzle chambers well ahead of their classmates.

Mix-and-Match Puzzle Chambers

The beauty of the #QRBreakIN reverse escape room is the versatility of the pedagogy and how quickly it allows you to offer on-the-spot feedback, drastically reducing the traditional routine of grading massive stacks of student work outside of school hours. The modular design lends itself easily to new school tech integration like Quizizz, Google Forms, EdPuzzle, and Flipgrid, while providing equal opportunity for teachers more accustomed to hands-on deliverables to make use of traditional classroom staples like Sketchnotes, graphic organizers, or timed small group conversations.

Let's take a closer look at some of the sample strategies and tech tools you can use when designing these bite-sized student centers. And if you're building your own #QRBreakIN, feel free to mix and match as many of these activities together (or add new ones) as you'd like!

EdPuzzle

The Chamber: A staple of "flipped" classroom instruction, EdPuzzle allows teachers the ability to take any existing video on the web (or make one of their own) and embed a check for understanding questions along the way. EdPuzzle simply won't let students progress to the next portion of the video before answering each of the prompt items provided.

The Escape: EdPuzzle does all the work for you in this center, as any video that you can find (or create) on their free website comes with its own custom URL (which you can turn into a QR code) to share with the group by printing it directly onto the center activity. Have each team member complete the EdPuzzle and call the teacher over to confirm your progress for a new center to complete. A simple spot check can suffice at this station, since each student's work will automatically be saved in a spreadsheet that you can review after class.

Flipgrid

The Chamber: A clever twist on interactive discussion, Flipgrid puzzles challenge an entire student team to work together. Responding to a content-specific prompt, the team records its answer in a two- to three-minute video.

The Escape: Student teammates need to work together to fill a full two-and-a-half- to three-minute-discussion prompt (on video), calling the teacher over after the video has been successfully uploaded to confirm their progress. The fact that the video submission will automatically be stored means that students will be that much more likely to take their conversation seriously. Teachers can spot check on the fly, and then go back in and review each video after class has ended to get a closer look at who's getting the hang of unit concepts and who might still be struggling.

Google Forms

The Chamber: Turn a simple open response question item into a "minimum number of characters required" writing prompt, using the response validation feature discussed in Chapter 7 to compel students to provide thoughtful writing samples of significant length.

The Escape: Response validation is a fantastic way to ensure that every student is submitting a work product of any specified length that you'd like. The Google Form automatically collects all submissions into a spreadsheet, so you have the ability to review the relative strength of each work product after class is through. Provide a QR code or URL to your Google Form at this station and ask all students to show you their success screens before moving on.

Microlab

The Chamber: Not quite the full-blown Microlab protocol we discussed in Chapter 5, this station is simply designed to make sure everybody in a group has had an equal opportunity to share their thoughts on a given topic. Once the group is ready, students call the teacher over for a five-minute chat about the assigned question, citing specific text evidence as necessary to add credibility and support to their argument.

The Escape: No technology required! The only way to escape this chamber is for an entire team to be prepared with solid text evidence to support a full five-minute dialogue. And that means *everybody* in the group should be prepared to contribute to the conversation—and the teacher reserves the right to extend the group's working time in the Microlab "penalty box" until it's clear that everybody in the chamber is on the same page.

Number Cruncher

The Chamber: This is a fun way to emphasize particular numbers of significance, even if you're not a math teacher. Example: the price of Jay Gatsby's Rolls Royce, the height of the Eiffel Tower, or the year of the Louisiana Purchase.

The Escape: This center will task students to complete a simple math problem. They'll need to solve an equation, where each of the variables are specific numbers of importance relating to your assigned text. When the group calls the teacher over to confirm, they'll either have the right answer or they won't. If they're good to go, they're rewarded with a new puzzle to solve. If not, it's two agonizing minutes in the penalty box to sit and reflect on where their math went wrong, which makes this a great way to help teach students the value of double (and triple!) checking their work.

Quizizz

The Chamber: Quizizz turns any multiple-choice assessment into an interactive arcade game with leaderboards and individual player awards for the highest scorers. But unlike the old-school coin-op quarter-eating video games, this is totally free! And if you don't like your score, you can simply play again.

The Escape: Upload any quiz to Quizizz (or browse the thousands that are already available on the site) and post the game link as a QR code or URL at this #QRBreakIn station. Teammates are welcome to talk to one another and strategize as they complete their Quizizz, but the group won't be allowed to leave the station until at least *two* team members have earned a perfect score. The website automatically allows students to take each test as many times as they'd like, which is a great way to test to mastery (87 percent on the first try? Take the Quizizz again to make your way to 100 percent!), and the collaborative approach to test-taking ensures that everybody in the group is working either as a player coach or as a test taker at any given time. Teachers also have the ability to go back and see how each player scored.

Gimkit

The Chamber: Gimkit puts a game-inspired twist on what otherwise could have been a simple flash card review activity. With Gimkit, students complete a self-paced online quiz by answering questions from a "kit" of digital cards. For each correct answer, the student earns in-game currency, which they can then invest back into the Gimkit shop to purchase scoring power-ups like more cash per question, streak bonuses, and insurance against wrong answers.

The Escape: Teachers can create a Gimkit homework assignment with a set threshold of earnings required from each student who attempts this challenge. Consider building a kit with just twenty review questions (great for vocab words) and setting an earnings goal of somewhere in the neighborhood of $1000 or more. As a default, each correct answer on the Gimkit platform only earns students $1 apiece to start the game—so you can guarantee that players will have to spend more than a few passes through the same question set, reviewing correct answers with teammates and strategizing together as they make their way to the target amount. The faster players invest in themselves, and the more questions they can get right, the sooner they'll reach the target amount required to clear this chamber.

Sketchnote

The Chamber: A sketchnote is an opportunity to create a visual representation of a text or concept. This offers a student the chance to imagine what newly discovered content might look like as a picture. Sketchnotes should always be scored on the level of detail that the student includes, *not* on their particular degree of artistic ability.

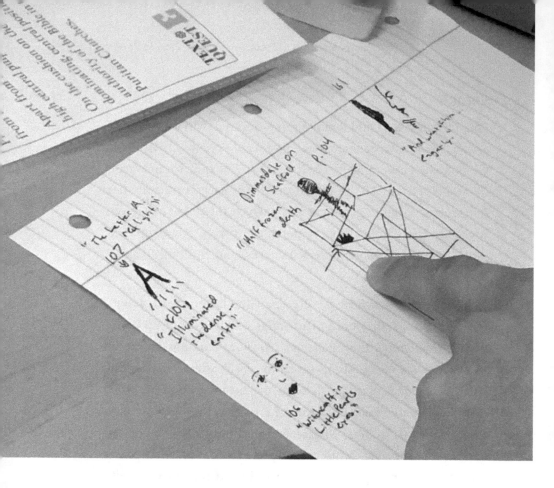

The Escape: No need for technology here. At a sketchnote center, student teams should be presented with the challenge to depict a concept or chunk of textual evidence as a drawing, annotating specific details that their image contains. Examples might include "draw the setting of this story," or "what does (person, character, or figure x) look like?" Make note that each sketch should include at least ten different annotations from the source material to account for any details that it includes, or they'll be trapped in the penalty box for a two-minute work product review before the team is eligible to resubmit.

Sporcle

The Chamber: A non-teaching tool with incredible application in your average classroom, Sporcle is an online trivia site with ready-made quizzes ranging from every topic under the sun, from World Series Champions by year to guessing the names of various countries simply by looking at the shapes of different geographical maps.

The Escape: Find a pertinent Sporcle quiz (or create your own) and share a QR code or URL for this station, where players have to work together to solve all questions provided in the linked quiz before time runs out. Placing Latin American countries on a map, sorting US Presidents in chronological order, or correctly matching vocabulary terms with their definitions are just a handful of the types of quizzes that this free site provides. Have teammates work together or as cooperating individuals to complete their trivia quiz, then call the teacher over when they're done. And if at first they don't succeed, rescan the QR code to try, try again!

Spotlight Performer

The Chamber: Think charades, but for school. Student teams must work together to re-enact a major concept, scene, or idea from the unit as a posed tableau or sixty-second song, rap, commercial, or skit.

The Escape: No need for a QR code here, but bring your camera! When the group is ready to take center stage as a team of Spotlight Performers, they'll simply call the teacher over and let their creativity fly. (Be sure to remind students that the penalty box is lying in wait if the work product isn't quite up to snuff.) So what does a DNA molecule look like as a human statue? Can you sing the Pythagorean Theorem to the tune of "Twinkle, Twinkle,

Little Star"? There are lots of laughs and memories to be made at this station, guaranteed.

Timeline Tally

The Chamber: Nothing fancy is here and no QR codes are needed; this is just your average timeline puzzle. Work together with your teammates to plot (x) number of items on a custom timeline. Timeline Tally is perfect for helping students keep track of important events and chronology.

The Escape: Teammates must work together to provide a timeline of events for the unit or course content in question, including at least (x) different items along their team's timeline. To make this station more challenging, simply provide the start and end dates of the timeline and leave it up to your students to determine the most important details that should fall along it. Let student groups know that you reserve the right to enforce two minutes in the penalty box if a particularly noteworthy event is omitted, which will help hold them accountable for generating higher quality work before calling you over to review it.

#TrendingTopic

The Chamber: This is not a real Twitter challenge, but it is a chance to distill unit content into contemporary #TrendingTopics to demonstrate mastery and understanding of course material.

The Escape: Students work together to develop at least five original tweets (with #hashtags), as if they're explaining to a friend what the heck was going on in the content they just studied. As an added bonus, have them develop at least one tweet written *completely in emojis*. Use the QR code at this station to link to a blank Google Doc, where students can write their "tweets" before calling you over to review. (Make sure to ask them to explain their choices.) Metacognition for the win!

REDLINING
A RAISIN IN THE SUN

Scan the QR Code

(RUTH points impatiently to the rolled up Tribune on the table, and he gets it and spreads it out and vaguely reads the front page)

WALTER: Set off another bomb yesterday.

Have all group members take handwritten notes on the Cicero Race Riots and the Illinois bombings of 1951. What stands out to you in this article? Make note of at least 10 items.

When each team member has completed your notes, call The Narrator over to review your lists. But if it's not up to par, you'll earn 2 minutes in the Penalty Box.

ENGLEWOOD

WEB**Q**UEST

TYPE C NEIGHBORHOOD
MORTGAGE: DECLINING

 QR Breakin

Webquest

The Chamber: As a gamified twist on article reading or "walking notes," a webquest chamber will task students to read an article related to unit content (linked in a QR code or URL), then provide a quick summary of the key points that they find.

The Escape: Find any article or web page related to your current unit of study and turn it into a QR code or URL. Student groups read it and provide a summary of the main ideas. Each student should provide an itemized list of at least ten key points (written in complete sentences) that they found in the source text. This is another puzzle where the penalty box comes in handy, as student groups who call the teacher over for review, without first having properly taken thorough notes on the source article (this includes putting a title on their notes, so they remain organized) can find themselves trapped in the two-minute penalty box at the teacher's discretion.

YouTube

The Chamber: Some unit concepts are simply better off when presented with video supplements. Whole class video instruction rarely works the way we hoped it would, often because something as innocent as a student cough or an untimely slammed locker in the hallway can result in an entire class missing a key piece of dialogue or information. For a YouTube chamber, teachers can include anything from a short video walkthrough of a particular chemical reaction to a staged recitation of Shakespeare. Have one team member scan the QR Code, and you've got a mini screening party.

The Escape: YouTube videos lend themselves perfectly to Cornell notes or graphic organizer type activities. Turn any YouTube video into a QR code or clickable link and have all members watch the video and complete (x) items on something like an FQR chart (a mix-and-match graphic organizer listing any "Facts," "Questions," and/or "Reactions" that it inspires). The team approach to the mini movie screening gives it a bit of social interaction, and the penalty box proviso gives teachers the discretion

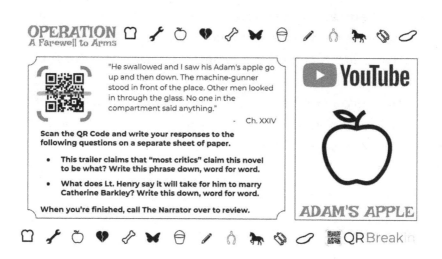

OPERATION
A Farewell to Arms

"He swallowed and I saw his Adam's apple go up and then down. The machine-gunner stood in front of the place. Other men looked in through the glass. No one in the compartment said anything."

- Ch. XXIV

Scan the QR Code and write your responses to the following questions on a separate sheet of paper.

- This trailer claims that "most critics" claim this novel to be what? Write this phrase down, word for word.

- What does Lt. Henry say it will take for him to marry Catherine Barkley? Write this down, word for word.

When you're finished, call The Narrator over to review.

▶ YouTube

ADAM'S APPLE

QR Break

to detain a group for an additional two-minute timeout if it looks like the group might have missed a key takeaway from the video.

The Bottom Line

More face time with students. More peer-to-peer collaboration. Deeper learning through bite-sized schema. Teaching to mastery. Faster feedback. Modular challenges for easy differentiation. A friendly sense of teamwork and competition. Clear icons with a cohesive visual theme to tie every puzzle together. And an infinite adaptability to any new tasks or technologies that might come your way.

Thanks to its high-energy appeal and student-centered approach to classroom instruction, the #QRBreakIN approach has completely replaced lectures in my classroom. Students learn in different ways on different days, and so we'll often stretch a single game across two or three consecutive days of instruction before we rally the entire class back together for a Socratic Seminar, so everyone can connect the dots and show off just how much they've learned. *Expelliarmus*, PowerPoint.

Questions for Discussion

1. Take a look at your typical slideshow. How much information does it contain? How often do students have to process more than seven new items of information at a time when it is presented to them?

2. Do you currently teach a unit that might lend itself easily to a #QRBreakIN centers style team competition? How could you use something like a multi-day centers activity as a springboard to a Socratic Seminar?

3. How much time do you typically spend creating a slideshow? What would happen if you divided the slides into printed chambers with smaller deliverable work products?

Chapter 9

Living Video Games and Game-Changing Escapes

On a sunny day, play outside.

—*Shigeru Miyamoto, Creator of* Super Mario
Brothers *and* The Legend of Zelda

It's Dangerous to Go Alone! Take This.

Think back to how many countless hours you spent in one of *Zelda*'s water temples. Or desperately trying to nail that perfect jump in *Super Mario Bros.* Unlike the traditional classroom, the video game experience doesn't punish you for taking all the time in the world to finesse that individual skill: It waits patiently for you to discover the secrets on your own. In fact, it's designed that way.

One of my favorite video game stories tells the tale of the early stages of development of the game that would go on to become the cornerstone for *The Legend of Zelda* franchise. Inspired by his own love of exploring caves and hillsides while collecting insects as a child, video game designer Shigeru Miyamoto (who had just come hot off the heels of a smash success of the original *Mario Brothers*) set out to design a game experience that rewarded free play and exploration in the style of Indiana Jones.

The problem? Early testers found the game experience confusing. Having grown accustomed to the fundamental gameplay mechanics of side-scrolling platformers like *Mario*, many players were not exactly sure what they were expected to do when armed with a miniature sprite who carried a trusty sword and the total freedom to navigate an overhead map in all directions at once.

So Miyamoto took away the sword.

Nathan Birch of Uproxx explains:

> *Miyamoto's logic was that making Zelda perplexing would force kids to share information with their friends and foster a sense of community around the game, and it worked! Anyone who spent any time on playgrounds during the '80s knows* The Legend of Zelda *was consistently one of the most discussed games.*

With its myriad of temple puzzles, unlockable secrets, and intertwining challenges, the *Zelda* franchise and so many video games like it function like a digital escape room. In *The Game Believes in You: How Digital Play Can Make Our Kids Smarter*, Greg Toppo points out the enduring appeal of these digital escapes, writing:

> *Games give you a chance to learn at your own pace, take risks, and cultivate deeper*

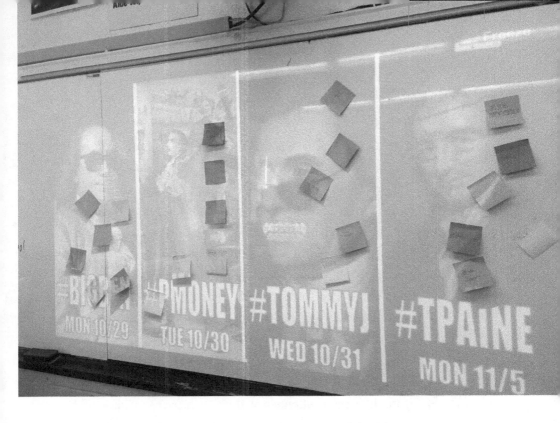

understanding. While teachers, parents, and friends may encourage and support you, these natural resources are limited. Computers work on a completely different scale and timetable. They're 'infinitely stupid and infinitely patient,' according to game designer Michael John. Your teacher may be overwhelmed, your friends wish you'd finish your homework. But ... a well-designed game sits and waits ... and waits. It doesn't care if that wearisome math problem takes you fifteen seconds or four hours. Do it again. Take all day. The game believes in you.

Though today's video games are infinitely more nuanced than their predecessors, four decades of virtual worlds can trace their origins back to the rudimentary quarter-munching arcade machines of yesteryear. They've literally been programmed to hook your attention. What would our classrooms look like if we could capture the same thrill that comes from the countless hours spent slogging through virtual dungeons?

- Display a "character select" menu of project choices to your overhead board and let students use sticky notes to stake their claim on which option appeals to them the most.
- Video games are loaded with collectible secrets and "Easter eggs." Use an augmented reality app to hide scannable content inside of traditional printed handouts.
- Use a free editing software or phone app like iMovie to create a "cut scene" or hype trailer for an upcoming unit of study. Or better yet, have this year's students create a trailer that you'll use to get *next* year's classes excited!
- Draft a "level select" choice board for the end-of-unit summative assessment where students have the power to navigate different challenges at their own pace, perhaps with the option to choose an essay, or a vlog post, or an in-class presentation, OR a traditional written test. You can even make a note of the projected difficulty of each assignment and require all students to select one assessment of each type before year's end.
- Bowser. Gannon. Mike Tyson. Any hero is only as memorable as his greatest adversary! Clearly defined bad guys help players identify a common enemy and work that much harder towards a shared goal. What epic stories could you dream up for a yearlong escape from the standardized exam kingdom ruled by the evil Negatron?
- Offer "extra lives" in the form of assessment retakes that can only be unlocked once students have completed a series of skill building challenges. In the *Mario* franchise, players earn an "extra life" for every 100 gold coins that they are successfully able to collect. How might your students benefit if they had the opportunity to retake a unit exam after

successfully completing a skill-building EdPuzzle or taking part in three consecutive study halls worth of extra help?

- Fire up a take-home Quizizz assignment (or Gimkit homework) where students have an open window of time to "play the game" as many times as they'd like in an effort to make it to the top of the digital leaderboard. And just like the SAT, only their highest score counts.
- Collaboration teaches teamwork and communication. Throw a curveball into a regularly scheduled assessment by turning any traditional exam into a "two-player" game.
- Offer your classes the opportunity to use the Creative Mode in existing games like *Minecraft* and give students the chance to play in a virtual sandbox, building limitless virtual worlds inspired by the rich details and characters of your course content.
- Create a "bonus level" question on any traditional assessment (or as a timed review for an upcoming test), where students simply write down as many things as they can think of about the current unit's content that *weren't* included on the printed exam. Don't announce a particular point value to this question and watch your students really dig deep into their own learning!

Video games offer powerful escapes to virtual realms of endless possibilities. For classrooms looking to escape the meat grinder of hackneyed academic routine, borrowing ideas from these virtual frontiers can help ignite young minds to see the true value of an education beyond the four walls of any building. As Greg Toppo explains:

> In the end, what may be most important is helping kids maintain a sense of balance, of not letting games become the only safe, reliable, and

rewarding part of their lives. When children ask for his autograph, Shigeru Miyamoto, the legendary Japanese designer who created the Super Mario games for Nintendo, often signs notes: "On a sunny day, play outside."

So here's one last idea for an #EDrenaline Rush you might consider for a sunny day of your own.

And it all started on a sunny day in October.

An Escape Three Decades in the Making

In the fall of 1988, Mrs. Nancy Miller's kindergarten classes from the Thomas B. Conley School took a wide-eyed group of about thirty students on their first ever class trip to the local United States Post Office in our little known town of Asbury, New Jersey (no relation to Springsteen's Asbury Park). We even had the opportunity to come prepared with a whopping 25¢ in our pint-sized pockets, along with a self-addressed envelope, so we could purchase our very own stamps and send pre-written letters back home to our families.

It was a pretty great day. When we got back to school the following morning, Mrs. Miller asked each of us to draw pictures of our favorite memory of the trip, which she then photocopied and stapled together into a massive coloring book for each student to take home as a keepsake. Naturally, my mom saved it.

This one is from my dear childhood friend Steven Ciccolella. You can tell we're friends because he made a point of drawing my little dude right beside his little dude (Sorry, Jimmy!).

Flip a few pages later, and my good buddy Matt McGowan (twenty-five years before he was the best man at my wedding) offered this Han Solo in Carbonite-like illustration of "the guy sorting the mail."

And here we are three pages later, and Yours Truly decided to share this little gem with the world: A freakishly tall Mrs. Miller watches carefully (looking like that creepy girl from *The Grudge*) as somebody plunks down some cold, hard cash to "get r stamps."

Obligatory potshots at the artistic prowess of my childhood friends aside, here's what I absolutely love about this assignment:

1. Quality Pre-Teaching

Judging from the details we thought to include in these illustrations, it's abundantly clear that we came to the Post Office prepared. Bringing money to purchase a stamp, having pre-addressed envelopes with pre-written letters to our own families' addresses. Those little touches go a long way, and it shows that a lot of time and planning went into getting us ready for our first ever, school-sponsored, classroom escape.

2. Student Choice

Looking at the captions that we provided, each of the students responded to the same question ("What do you remember most about our trip?"), and we were given free rein to reflect on the experience in any way that we wanted to. What a powerful way to model for us as young learners that not every student will learn the same thing, let alone the same way, on the same day!

3. Scaffolded Teacher Support

Look at Steven's illustration. He depicted a number of his classmates standing right there outside the bus beside him. With a little bit of teacher help, he was able to make a list of the names of the people who he traveled in a close group with for the day's field trip. And the fact that Mrs. Miller collected individual illustrations from each of us upon our return from the trip and then compiled them into a class coloring book was a cool way to extend the learning beyond a single-day affair.

4. Learning Through Exploration

Matt's illustration is completely different from Steven's or mine. Instead of drawing a wide angle shot, Matt opted to zoom in close on a particular person that we'd met on our trip. He was clearly impressed by this postal employee and his staggering wall of sorting boxes. As a teacher, I absolutely love it that Mrs. Miller let both these "close ups" and the larger "scenes" make their way into the printed book.

5. Shared Work Products and the Freedom to Fail

Check out the difference between the caption on my page and those of my classmates. See how theirs are all spelled correctly in an easy-to-read teacher handwriting? Now take a look at my masterpiece. That's a gutsy teacher move right there, to give a child the freedom to fail even when they know that the student's work product will be going on display for all of the classmates (and the classmates' families!) to see. The fact that Mrs. Miller gave us the option to have teacher help *or* to brave this assignment solo is an awesome witness to her student-centered pedagogy. Furthermore, five-year-old me must have felt like a million bucks as a kid, writing and illustrating *an entire page of a printed book all by myself!*—even if adult me is all too painfully aware of the basic spelling error.

Bottom line: When done right, class trips are an outstanding addition to any classroom "escape" kit arsenal. Experiential, non-linear learning taps into a child's innate sense of curiosity and wonder, encouraging "free play" and discovery, and rewards students with the power to unlock new knowledge through exploration. In *Siddhartha,* Herman Hesse recalls the wisdom of the Buddha, noting, "Knowledge can be conveyed, but not wisdom. It can be found, it can be lived, it is possible to be carried by it, miracles can be performed with it, but it cannot be expressed in words and taught." For all the knowledge even the greatest teachers can impart, field trips remind us of the unparalleled wisdom that only comes from experience.

The Craziest Field Trip You've Ever Seen

Thirty years after our trip to the post office, I had the chance to organize a class trip of my own that borrows heavily from the lessons I learned from Mrs. Miller's original class outing. It also really pulls together just about every one of the threads we've discussed. It's a full-blown #EDrenaline Rush, where students have the freedom to wonder, explore, and discover the world-changing power to create and connect authentic learning experiences with the world around them. I think it's the perfect capstone to close out this book.

Comprehensive unit theming that draws inspiration from the texts and content for study? Check.

Theme park-like academic environments where students become explorers in their own educational adventures? You betcha.

Student-centered pedagogy driven by authentic opportunities for choice and non-linear learning? Big time.

Living video games with "big bad bosses" and thematic escapes from the traditional classroom? Okay then—here we go!

I double checked the phone number and dialed.

"Trans-Allegheny Lunatic Asylum. How can I help you?"

The Trans-Allegheny Lunatic Asylum is located in Weston, West Virginia, approximately four hours from my school. The hospital's main building is the second largest hand-cut sandstone structure in the world, trailing only the Kremlin in Moscow.

Formerly known as the West Virginia Hospital for the Insane and later as the Weston State Hospital, the site was designated a National Historic Landmark in 1990. It is one of only a handful of Kirkbride style mental institutions remaining in the United States to offer guided tours to the public. (And, if you're a believer in ghost stories, it is also rumored to be one of the most haunted places in the world.)

Opened in 1864 and intended to house just 250 patients in the solitude of its 26.5 acre footprint and ominous 666 acre campus, the hospital held 717 patients by 1880; 1,661 in 1938; over 1,800 in 1949; and, at its peak, 2,600 in overcrowded conditions in the 1950s before it was forcibly closed in 1994, due to mandated reforms in the care of disabilities and mental health. It stands today as a powerful reminder of the history and treatment of mental illness in

our country and offers a fascinating glimpse into the very real living conditions that inspired many of the most brilliant minds and provocative works in American literature.

"Hi. I'm a high school teacher in Arlington, Virginia," I said awkwardly. "Are you guys open for school group tours?"

It was worth a shot. My class had nearly completed a full year studying a survey of American literature, including Southern Gothic authors like Flannery O'Connor and William Faulkner. We'd learned all about the hauntings and horrors of Victorian manors from seminal works like Edgar Allan Poe's "The Fall of the House of Usher" and Charlotte Perkins Gilman's "The Yellow Wall-Paper." And we'd spent months discussing the troubled history of authors struggling with mental health issues like Sylvia Plath, Ernest Hemingway, and Zelda Fitzgerald.

"You bet!" the voice on the other end of the line responded. "In fact, the asylum is closed to the public on Mondays. And we would love to have you! You'll have the grounds all to yourselves!"

Once I received the go-ahead from my principal, I finalized logistics with my ridiculously talented colleague, Carleen Knauf (@carleenonme), who teaches two other sections of the same American Literature class. Together, we submitted a request for two charter buses and set about planning our trip—right after we put together a quick video game-inspired iMovie trailer to screen for each of our class sections to help introduce this one-of-a-kind classroom escape.

Scan here to check out the trailer video for our asylum field trip.

I've never seen a group of students so excited.

High-energy class trips are a profound and powerful way to inspire lifetime learners. While not every class escape activity has to be as wild as a trip with over one hundred students (plus parents, administrators, and school counselors) to an abandoned insane asylum—the pedagogy behind this outing is firmly grounded in the exact same spirit of using your course content and a bit of outside inspiration to create lasting academic memories.

Do You Wanna Build an Asylum?

In lieu of a traditional written end-of-course assessment for our final exam, I put a twenty-first-century spin on Mrs. Miller's Post Office Book: Students were tasked with using Google Sites to create their very own tailor-made insane asylums and "committing" any one character that we had encountered throughout the entire year's worth of study. And that meant open season on everything from futuristic cyber prisons for Guy Montag of *Fahrenheit 451* to Puritan penal colonies of shame and isolation for *The Scarlet Letter*'s Hester Prynne.

But more than simply perpetuating a barbaric historical malpractice onto a hapless character from American literature, students were challenged to present a three-dimensional view of asylum life from multiple perspectives throughout their projects, synthesizing all sorts of writing and rhetorical strategies by crafting a series of individual web pages on their site such as:

- **A Landing Page** that speaks specifically to the unique amenities and features of this particular asylum (with inspiration drawn specifically from the source text of the characters who might be so unfortunate as to inhabit it).
- **A Patient's Diary**, in which the students assume the persona of the helpless character from fiction who had received this terrible sentence. Students write a series of journal entries

(in character) about this warped new world in which they find themselves and how it compares to the life that this individual once knew outside the asylum's massive walls.

- **A Doctor's Note**, in which students attempt to see the world from the eyes of a period-appropriate physician, citing "the latest research" (much of it now debunked) and using their powers of rhetoric to make the case for why a medical professional in the time period of this work of fiction might have argued for this patient's commitment to such an extreme course of action.

- **A Contemporary Perspective** requires students to cite extensive new medical knowledge (like the DSM-V) to offer a more informed diagnosis of the particular patient in question in light of how the same character might be perceived thanks to twenty-first-century breakthroughs in medicine and psychology, ultimately making the case for alternate forms of treatment to restore and affirm the dignity of these individuals who might otherwise have been so easily discarded.

- **A Personal Reflection** allows students to offer personal thoughts on all they learned through this immersive project and the uncharted break from the traditional academic routine. Bar none, this section, more than any, illustrated just how powerful and resonant an experience this ambitious "escape" project truly had been.

If you're interested, head over to EDrenalineRush.com/Resources to check out a sample asylum inspired by this once-in-a-lifetime escape from a traditional final assessment. I'd like to give the last word of this chapter to the students and chaperones who helped make this trip such a resounding success:

I wanted to thank you for including me on the field trip. The kids were so good; you obviously didn't need me there. It was fascinating, and I found my thoughts this morning turning constantly to what I had seen—especially all those long hallways, that peeling paint . . .

If the goal is to teach the kids to think, I cannot think of a more thought-provoking place. And I was very interested in your discussion with (our dean of academics) about how it can be tied into teaching about the dignity of the human person. What was disturbing about the place was the thought of how so many people suffered there. But that was not the intent of such a carefully constructed place (at least the original building). So the discussion of how it got to be a place of neglect is so important. Of course, not everything that happened there was bad, not everyone suffered. Medical trends followed cultural trends, public v. private institutions (funding), human nature—both good and bad; does the end justify the means . . . you have everything there! And all so relevant: Healthcare reform is in the news still every day. We cannot move forward without examining our past. Something so meaty, to be worthwhile, deserves time to prepare and reflect.

—Sara Sullivan, parent chaperone and
member of the board of trustees

Going to the asylum and listening to the tour guide was super insightful. It was crazy listening to the guide and hearing the history of the asylum. I was definitely shocked and was not expecting to hear the stuff we learned but feel much more educated about the topic now. It was really eye-opening. It shows you things you would never even think of. I would say it is almost sickening in a way to see how terrible the treatment of these patients was but amazing to see how far mental health has developed since then.

This trip was awesome. It was something I would never have done on my own, but I can now say I have thanks to this experience. It definitely was something that only affects you fully by going and being there, rather than just reading about it. Can I come back next year???

—Jennifer J., Bishop O'Connell
High School Class of 2018

I'd like to think Mrs. Miller would be proud.

Questions for Discussion

1. Do you have a favorite video game? How might you adapt some of the same elements from this game for use in your classroom?

2. How might a "player versus player" or "good versus evil" video game-like twist enhance an existing unit or assessment in your course content?

3. What sort of "sunny day" field trip could you take to provide your students with an authentic classroom escape experience to enrich and enhance everything they have been studying?

Conclusion

You Can Go Your Own Way

After nine chapters of communist classroom takeovers, high-energy obstacle courses, and tailor-made insane asylums, we've officially come to the end of our journey. Together, we've braved haunted mansions, conquered barbed wire mazes, vanquished PowerPoint quicksand, and discovered the top-secret blueprints for building our very own class escape rooms. My hope is that you'll walk away from this adventure with a jam-packed teacher toolbox full of exciting new strategies and instructional approaches to help you change the game in your schools and classrooms, regardless of your grade level or content area.

But our #EDrenaline Rush is really just beginning.

Theme parks transport us to magical, far-off worlds where it feels like anything is possible, while obstacle course races and escape rooms push participants to dig deep inside themselves and work with their teammates to tackle extreme challenges and unlock untold levels of potential. My goal throughout this book has been to share some of these same examples from my own life and career in an effort to encourage you to take the next steps and make use of them in your own schools and classrooms. Feel free to steal anything and everything contained in its pages. Head to EDrenalineRush.com for templates and please don't hesitate even for a second to "escape" from the playbook and instructional design I've provided to put your own creative twist on any of these techniques in any way that serves the unique needs of your students and your course content. Great teaching is a lifetime commitment to reflection and reinvention, and I can't wait to see what you come up with.

Find me on Twitter @MeehanEDU or join the #EDrenaline conversation online to share how your classes are doing amazing things to add life and energy to the traditional classroom. Theme park junkies, Mudders, or just good old-fashioned education butt-kickers: I'm proud to be a part of your tribe! Thank you from the bottom of my heart for inviting me along for the ride.

Thanks

Think where man's glory most begins and ends, and say my glory was I had such friends.

—William Butler Yeats,
"The Municipal Gallery Revisited"

I wanted to offer up some specific thank-yous, shout-outs, and acknowledgments to my incredible support network of friends, family members, Beta Testers, colleagues, and feedback rock stars, who've spent hundreds of hours between them reviewing, revising, and re-imagining all of the crazy ideas I'm able to dream up. I stand in their debt.

To my mom, a retired classroom teacher with more than two decades of experience: I'm sorry I ever doubted you, even for a second, for leaving television production behind to pursue a career in teaching. I get it now. It's not about the money, and it never was. You're the best teacher I've ever met.

To my dad, who coached rec sports and served as scoutmaster for some of the most formative extracurricular activities of my childhood: For teaching me the transformational power of motivation and for teaching me to be a man, even if we never quite managed to get me to learn how to drive a stick. Thanks for believing in me.

To my brothers, Jeremy and Josh: Jeremy, with a work ethic for an average day that most people would kill to have in a lifetime, and Josh, with a free-spirited sense of exploration that is truly a thing of wonder—thanks for having my back, guys. But I'm still the tallest. And it's in print now, so it's official.

To Dave and Shelley Burgess, Adam Welcome, George Couros, and Michael Matera: Thank you for your wisdom, support, and inspiration. To my Gates Foundation TAC peeps, my friends at ASCD, Carl, Meghan, the igKnight team and my O'Connell crew, my dear Crossland friends Kat and Levy, my fellow Catholic schoolteacher besties in Michael and Julia, my spiritual lifelines in Father Benetti, Pokey and Fitz, and my podcast buddies Russo and Dale—you guys make me proud to call myself a teacher. Steel sharpens steel. Thanks for all of the ideas that I've blatantly stolen from your classrooms over the years.

To the many classroom teachers who helped inspire the educator that I am today: Thank you for your incredible example. I like to think of my teaching style as a Frankenstein hybrid of all the greatest hits that I had the privilege of seeing from Mrs. Nancy Miller, Mrs. Joan Bradshaw, and Ms. Sheila Riddle of the Thomas B. Conley School; Mr. Donald Dwyer, Mr. Chip Riddle, and Mrs. Carolyn Smith of Ethel Hoppock Middle School; Mr. Vincent Angeline, Mr. David Lockhart, Ms. Cathy Long, and Mr. Keith Parent of North Hunterdon High School; and Dr. Michael Mack and Dr. Christopher Wheatley of The Catholic University of America. They say that your favorite class is the one that you like the most, but your best class is the one where you learn the most.

You folks were the best of the best, and I am so grateful to have been a student in your classrooms.

To the hundreds of students I've had the honor of teaching since starting this crazy journey in what seems like both a lifetime and just an instant ago: Thanks for letting me create a sandbox for you and showing me all of the cool castles you guys could build. Thanks to Walt Disney for teaching me how to dream.

And last on this list but first in all things I do, to my wife, Laura, a world-class educator by day and an actual rock star musician by night: Thanks for the countless times you've let me pick your brain before you've had your first cup of coffee. You're the reason I'm excited to wake up in the morning and the beating heart behind everything that I do throughout the day. Thanks for your patience, for giving me someone to look up to, and for your tireless support.

This book is for you.

Bibliography

"About." *National Blogging Collaborative*. nationalblog-gingcollaborative.com/about.

Aristotle. *The Metaphysics*. Amhurst, NY: Prometheus Books, 1991.

Birch, Nathan. "20 Fascinating Facts You May Not Know About 'The Legend Of Zelda'." *UPROXX*. Oct. 15, 2014. uproxx.com/viral/15-fascinating-facts-you-may-not-know-about-the-legend-of-zelda.

Bohm, David, and Lee Nichol. *On Dialogue*. New York: Routledge, 2004.

Chou, Yu-Kai. *Actionable Gamification: Beyond Points, Badges, and Leaderboards*. Fremont: Octalysis Media, 2016.

Couros, George. *The Innovator's Mindset: Empower Learning, Unleash Talent, and Lead a Culture of Creativity*. San Diego: Dave Burgess Consulting, Inc., 2015.

"Crossland High in Temple Hills, Maryland." *Crossland High in Temple Hills, MD | StartClass*. public-schools.startclass.com/l/41047/Crossland-High-in-Temple-Hills-Maryland.

Hesse, Hermann. *Siddhartha*. New York: Random House, 1981.

Howes, Lewis. "20 Lessons from Walt Disney on Entrepreneurship, Innovation and Chasing Your Dreams." *Forbes*, 19 July 2012, forbes.com/sites/lewishowes/2012/07/17/20-business-quotes-and-lessons-from-walt-disney/#7dcb1b994ba9.

"In Walt's Own Words: Plussing Disneyland." *The Walt Disney Family Museum*, 9 Oct. 2015, waltdisney.org/blog/walts-own-words-plussing-disneyland.

Kinni, Theodore B. *Be Our Guest: Perfecting the Art of Customer Service*. Glendale, CA: Disney Editions, 2011.

Knight, Jim. *Unmistakable Impact: a Partnership Approach for Dramatically Improving Instruction*. Thousand Oaks: Corwin, 2011.

Kuang, Cliff. "Disney's $1 Billion Bet on a Magic Wristband." *Wired*, 10 March 2015. wired.com/2015/03/disney-magicband.

Lemov, Doug. *Teach Like a Champion 2.0: 62 Techniques that Put Students on the Path to College 2nd Edition*. San Francisco: Jossey-Bass, 2015.

Lewis, Sarah. *The Rise: Creativity, the Gift of Failure, and The Search for Mastery*. New York: Simon & Schuster, 2014.

McDougall, Christopher. *Born to Run: A Hidden Tribe, Superathletes, and the Greatest Race the World Has Never Seen*. New York: Vintage Books, 2009.

McKee, Robert. *Story: Substance, Structure, Style and the Principles of Screenwriting*. New York: Regan Books, 1998.

Meehan, John. "5 Minute PD: 'Too Often We Confuse 'Dialogue' and 'Discussion' – and There's a Critical Difference between the Two.'" *Facebook*. Feb. 24, 2017. facebook.com/notes/teacher2teacher/too-often-we-confuse-dialogue-and-discussion-and-theres-a-critical-difference-be/849854778489063/.

Meet the Robinsons. Directed by Stephen Anderson. 2007. Burbank, CA: Walt Disney Pictures, 2007. DVD.

"Oh God, Teacher Arranged Desks In Giant Circle." Local. *The Onion*. Apr. 13, 2015. local.theonion.com/oh-god-teacher-arranged-desks-in-giant-circle-1819577697.

"Peer Discussion Improves Student Performance With 'Clickers'." *Science Daily.* Jan. 12, 2009. sciencedaily. com/releases/2009/01/090102100234.htm.

Perez, A.J. "Obstacle races going mainstream, more popular than marathons." *USA Today*, 2 November 2015. amp. usatoday.com/amp/73743474.

Schell, Jesse. *The Art of Game Design: A Book of Lenses.* Burlington: Morgan Kaufman, 2008.

Schmich, Mary. "Advice, like youth, probably just wasted on the young." *Chicago Tribune* (Chicago, IL), June 1997. web.archive.org/web/20051205053227/chicagotribune. com/news/columnists/chi-970601sunscreen,0,4664776. column?page=2.

Steinbeck, John. ". . . Like Captured Fireflies." *James M. Dourgarian, Bookman.* jimbooks.com/steinbeckephemera.htm.

Sylt, Christian. "The Secrets Behind Disney's $2.2 Billion Theme Park Profits." *Forbes Magazine*, 14 July 2014, forbes.com/sites/csylt/2014/07/14/the-secrets-behind-disneys-2-2-billion-theme-park-profits/#1d80aae0584f.

Toppo, Greg. *The Game Believes in You: How Digital Play Can Make Our Kids Smarter.* New York: St. Martin's Press, 2015.

Vestal, Andrew (September 14, 2000). "The History of Zelda". *GameSpot. (Page 174)*

Walker, Derek. *Animated Architecture.* New York: St. Martin's Press, 1982.

Weimer, Maryellen Weimer. "More Evidence That Active Learning Trumps Lecturing." *Faculty Focus* (blog). June 3, 2015, facultyfocus.com/articles/teaching-professor-blog/more-evidence-that-active-learning-trumps-lecturing.

Wiggins, Alexis. *The Best Class You Never Taught: How Spider Web Discussion Can Turn Students into Learning Leaders.* Alexandria: ASCD, 2017.

Wynter, Amanda. "Bringing Twitter to the Classroom." Education. *The Atlantic.* Sept. 15, 2014. theatlantic.com/education/archive/2014/09/the-case-for-having-class-discussions-on-twitter/379777.

"You Can Make the Impossible Happen...Again." *ALS Association.* 2019. alsa.org/fight-als/ice-bucket-challenge.html.

More from

DAVE **B**URGESS
Consulting, Inc.

Since 2012, DBCI has been publishing books that
inspire and equip educators to be their best. For
more information on our DBCI titles or to purchase
bulk orders for your school, district, or book study,
visit **DaveBurgessConsulting.com/DBCIBooks**.

More from the *Like a PIRATE*™ Series

Teach Like a PIRATE by Dave Burgess

Explore Like a Pirate by Michael Matera

Learn Like a Pirate by Paul Solarz

Play Like a Pirate by Quinn Rollins

Run Like a Pirate by Adam Welcome

Lead Like a PIRATE™ Series

Lead Like a PIRATE by Shelley Burgess and Beth Houf

Balance Like a Pirate by Jessica Cabeen, Jessica Johnson,
and Sarah Johnson

Lead with Culture by Jay Billy

Lead with Literacy by Mandy Ellis

Lead beyond Your Title by Nili Bartley

Leadership & School Culture

Culturize by Jimmy Casas

Escaping the School Leader's Dunk Tank by Rebecca Coda
and Rick Jetter

The Innovator's Mindset by George Couros

Kids Deserve It! by Todd Nesloney and Adam Welcome

Let Them Speak! by Rebecca Coda and Rick Jetter

Start. Right. Now. by Todd Whitaker, Jeffrey Zoul, and
  Jimmy Casas

Stop. Right. Now. by Jimmy Casas and Jeffrey Zoul Jetter

The Limitless School by Abe Hege and Adam Dovico

The Pepper Effect by Sean Gaillard

The Principled Principal by Jeffrey Zoul and
  Anthony McConnell

The Secret Solution by Todd Whitaker, Sam Miller, and
  Ryan Donlan

They Call Me "Mr. De" by Frank DeAngelis

Unmapped Potential by Julie Hasson and Missy Lennard

Your School Rocks by Ryan McLane and Eric Lowe

Technology & Tools

50 Things You Can Do with Google Classroom by Alice Keeler
  and Libbi Miller

50 Things to Go Further with Google Classroom by Alice Keeler
  and Libbi Miller

140 Twitter Tips for Educators by Brad Currie, Billy Krakower,
  and Scott Rocco

Code Breaker by Brian Aspinall

Creatively Productive by Lisa Johnson

Google Apps for Littles by Christine Pinto and Alice Keeler

Master the Media by Julie Smith

Shake Up Learning by Kasey Bell

Social LEADia by Jennifer Casa-Todd

Teaching Math with Google Apps by Alice Keeler and
  Diana Herrington

Teaching Methods & Materials

All 4s and 5s by Andrew Sharos

Ditch That Homework by Matt Miller and Alice Keeler

Ditch That Textbook by Matt Miller

Educated by Design by Michael Cohen

The EduProtocol Field Guide by Marlena Hebern and
 Jon Corippo

Instant Relevance by Denis Sheeran

LAUNCH by John Spencer and A.J. Juliani

Make Learning MAGICAL by Tisha Richmond

Pure Genius by Don Wettrick

Shift This! by Joy Kirr

Spark Learning by Ramsey Musallam

Sparks in the Dark by Travis Crowder and Todd Nesloney

Table Talk Math by John Stevens

The Classroom Chef by John Stevens and Matt Vaudrey

The Wild Card by Hope and Wade King

The Writing on the Classroom Wall by Steve Wyborney

Inspiration, Professional Growth, & Personal Development

The Four O'Clock Faculty by Rich Czyz

Be REAL by Tara Martin

Be the One for Kids by Ryan Sheehy

The EduNinja Mindset by Jennifer Burdis

Empower Our Girls by Lynmara Colon and Adam Welcome

How Much Water Do We Have? by Pete and Kris Nunweiler

P Is for Pirate by Dave and Shelley Burgess

The Path to Serendipity by Allyson Apsey

Through the Lens of Serendipity by Allyson Apsey

Sanctuaries by Dan Tricarico

Shattering the Perfect Teacher Myth by Aaron Hogan
Stories from Webb by Todd Nesloney
Talk to Me by Kim Bearden
The Zen Teacher by Dan Tricarico

Children's Books

Dolphins in Trees by Aaron Polansky
The Princes of Serendip by Allyson Apsey

Bring the #EDRENALINE RUSH to Your School or Event!

John Meehan offers game-changing keynotes, workshops, and professional development programs. He leads with passion and believes enthusiasm is infectious—because the big secret of education is that we don't teach content, but we use content to teach people. His heartfelt and high-energy approach to student-centered instruction adds life and energy to any course or content area, and his dynamic presentations offer practical strategies for teachers, so they can leave lectures in the dust and become an "Impresario with a Scenario" at any grade level.

What People Are Saying about John Meehan

"This session blew my mind!! Everything about it was great—amazing ideas that I am 100% going to work to implement in my building. Thank you for sharing your story and your work!"

"His energy was contagious! I just wish my teachers could see him."

"The best session I have ever been to! So informative and motivating. Highly recommend."

"John is a dynamic presenter! I could really sense his passion for making learning fun."

Popular Messages from John Meehan

John's presentations can be tailored to your event. Here's a handful of keynote sessions he's presented in the past:

- Game Changing Student Engagement
- Gamification Basics for Any Grade Level
- Designing REVERSE Escape Rooms with #QRBreakIN
- Adapting Fantasy Sports for Everyday Classrooms
- Microcredentials > Micromanagement for Self-Guided PD

Connect

Connect with John Meehan for more information about bringing him to your event.

john@edrenalinerush.com

EDrenalineRush.com

@MeehanEDU

About the Author

John Meehan is an English teacher and school instructional coach at Bishop O'Connell High School in Arlington, Virginia. He began his journey as a teacher in 2010 as a career switcher through The New Teacher Project, after spending five years working in social media and event marketing. He is a 2017 ASCD Emerging Leader and an alumnus of the 2016–2018 Bill & Melinda Gates Foundation Teacher Advisory Council. In 2016, he was named one of the "40 Under 40" of Arlington, Virginia, by the Leadership Center for Excellence. He is a past presenter and regular attendee at educational conferences throughout the United States, including the annual conference for National Catholic Education Association, ASCD Empower19, and the Play Like a Champion Today: Character Education Through Sports summer conference at the University of Notre Dame. He's an avid runner who's completed more than three dozen marathons, half marathons, long-distance road relays, mud runs, and obstacle course races. John lives in Silver Spring, Maryland, with his wife, Laura, a high school music teacher and fellow graduate of The Catholic University of America, and a giant-sized Maine Coon cat named Jack.

Connect with John:

EDrenalineRush.com | @MeehanEDU

About the Author